The Man in the Black Fur Coat

A Soldier's Adventures on the Eastern Front

By Oskar Scheja
As told by Dan Chiariello

ISBN 978-1499285239

This book is dedicated to my extended family, spread out across the globe and through history. It is part of my quest to discover them and preserve their memories so that I may enrich my understanding of who I am.

Contents

The Man in the
Black Fur Coat

INTRODUCTION

I called him Uncle Oskar but he wasn't really my uncle. Oskar lived with my mother's aunt Hedwig, or Tanta Hedy as we would say. The two had met in the mid 1950's and it wasn't long before they began living together. They spent the rest of their lives as a couple but were never married. Could I really call him my uncle? I always have, and so I will in this story.

My mother was born in 1940 in Gelsenkirchen, a small town in Germany's industrial area in the Ruhr Valley. She grew up in war-torn Europe and was raised by her mother Johanna, father Matthias, and her aunt Hedy. Hedy was very close with her sister, Johanna, and had become a second mother to my mom. Hedy had been married briefly to a man named Walter but I don't really know much about him or how he fell out of the picture. In the early 1950's Hedy left Germany for America and found a place to live near Newark, New Jersey. She met Oskar in a social club for German citizens living in the U.S. and the two moved in together. A few years later they relocated to an apartment in Bridgeport, Connecticut. They lived there for many more years before returning to Germany in the early 1970's. Hedy and Oskar settled in a small town called Vechta which sits in the northwestern part of the country. The land is flat, covered by fields of peat moss and pastures, a region where in many villages the horses and cows outnumber the people.

My grandmother at the time was living alone in Gelsenkirchen after my grandfather passed away. She soon moved into her own small apartment in Vechta to be near her sister. That is where they spent the rest of their lives.

My mother came to the States in the early nineteen sixties and stayed with her aunt in New Jersey. She met my father soon thereafter. I was born in New Jersey in 1964, and my two brothers soon followed. My mother remained very close to her aunt, after Hedy and Oskar moved to Bridgeport, and our family would travel up to their apartment in Connecticut to visit them from time to time. Uncle Oskar was always there but as I recall he mostly remained part of the background. He was quiet and best described as a very proud man. You could tell that when he was younger he must have been strong and solid, but as he entered his sixties that solid look had begun to melt away into something that was more like "stout". His hair was thin and speckled with intermittent black and white wisps. His eyes never opened too widely, conveying a sense of aloofness. I rarely recall him laughing, even when he seemed to be enjoying himself. When I think back I picture him in his red smoking jacket sitting in his master's chair in the living room, upright with perfect posture, a White Owl cigar between his lips. His chair sat next to a radio that was not some small, hand-held device, but instead a piece of furniture the size of a dresser. He listened to it for hours. The sound was always turned down so low that I could not tell if he were listening to music or discussion. It was his corner of the room. When we came to visit we tried not to disturb him, not because we were instructed to do so but instead out of a feeling that he required his private space.

From time to time he would become aware of an "isn't that so, Oskar?" emanating from the other side of the room near the kitchen where my mother and aunt where chatting over coffee and a piece of dry marble cake. That was usually followed by a "Was sagt ihr?" and one of them would repeat the question in German. He made his contribution to the conversation in a deliberate and commanding tone, as if it carried the utmost importance. This exchange in a loud, foreign language would interrupt the activity that my brother and I were engaged in. Oskar would glance in our direction, offer a wink or a secret smile, and then fade again into his chair by the radio. We knew not what was said, but we understood that he was proud of what he had to offer.

When I was thirteen years old my family moved to Vechta to spend two years in Germany. My parents wished to provide me and my brothers the opportunity to experience a different culture, and also to become closer with my mother's family. We rented the middle unit of a newly constructed row of three connected houses in a neighborhood of many homes and apartments that were arranged in geometric order with little space between them. That's what we saw from the front door. Stepping out of the kitchen door in the back, you walked straight into a cow pasture. To the left behind the row of houses on our street there was a field of kohlrabi, and to the right of the cow pasture the farmer grew winter wheat.

Hedy and Oskar lived further down on the same road but a few months after we arrived they moved in to the unit next to us. Looking back, I would think that afforded me the opportunity to really get to know Oskar, but somehow it didn't. My days were busy with school, making new friends, riding my bike, playing soccer with the neighborhood boys, and generally doing what thirteen year old kids do. I saw Oskar quite often as he and Tanta Hedy joined us for many meals, but he was just as quiet and just as proud.

Oskar took a walk every day as part of his regimen. On rare occasions I would join him. He walked with a cane, and did so with a gate that looked professionally choreographed. It was four-step process: the cane goes back, it swings forward, and then it is pressed firmly on the ground and held for the next stride. It exemplified the manner in which he performed everything, with an element of order and discipline. He spoke very little. The discussions we had were usually limited to a description of how quickly the neighborhood was changing. We left Germany after two years and moved back into our home in New Jersey. Oskar passed away not long thereafter.

Hedy lived in the apartment alone for many years after Oskar's death. She died in nineteen ninety. My mother flew to Germany to settle Hedy's affairs and returned with a few items she reserved for me. There were pictures, a collection of post cards, and an old note pad with over a hundred pages of writing. It was signed by Oskar Scheja and was believed to be his personal account of his experiences during World War Two.

The pages of the journal were still neat and so white that it was hard to believe the date that featured prominently on the first page stated "February 10, 1946". The binding was intact, and not a single page was torn. It looked as though it had hardly ever been opened. I was sure it contained a fascinating story. Family legend had it that he was part of the campaign on the Eastern Front, had been captured by the Russians, and escaped from a POW camp. I wanted very much to read it someday. I felt I owed it to the book, or more appropriately that I owed it to Oskar for taking so much care to record his story and preserve it so well. I made several attempts to do so but each time I never got past the first few words. It wasn't the language that kept me from doing so; my obstacle was that I was unable to read his handwriting. Though it was written very neatly it was penned in an old German handwriting style which I later learned is called "Sütterlin". Many of the letters were not recognizable to me. My mother, who was born in Germany, couldn't read it, and neither could my son's German teachers. The journal seemed destined to remain simply a family artifact. It lay undisturbed in a cabinet in our basement for over twenty years; the pages stayed white, the story unread and unappreciated.

The journal's fortune changed a few years ago when my wife and I grew increasingly interested in our collection of family pictures. Using digital photo archiving tools allowed us to organize photographs and arrange them in books to be printed. We proceeded to catalogue our current digital pictures, scan the printed ones, and gather them in a database. From these we created a printed album for each year. The albums contained not only the pictures but other snippets of our experiences from that year, such as stories, school art work, ticket stubs, and other memorabilia. We started with the present and continued going back in time. Eventually we hope to create a complete a digital and printed archive of our lives through pictures and stories.

My mother was moving out of her house around this time and recognized the opportunity existed for her to free herself from several large boxes of old family photographs that had been occupying a lot of space in her basement.

Taking advantage of my newly discovered appreciation of family artifacts she threatened to simply throw them out before I stepped in and took the lot. My father was quite fond of the cameras that he owned and loved taking pictures. There were a few thousand of them dating back to the 1940s. Some of the faces were familiar, my aunts, uncles and cousins, but many were not. My father isn't alive to help me recognize the people or describe the events. I soon discovered that I must reverse course and start with the oldest pictures while there are still people around who could help me.

Not only did I scan the old pictures and label them as well as I could, I also continued on with other artifacts. These included a collection of my father's poetry, digitally converting eight millimeter movies, wire reel audio recordings, and a diary of a trip my dad took to Europe in 1957. I was determine to create a lasting treasure for my children so that they may look at the collection and really know their family history.

The volume of work makes this a project that will take many years to complete. I regard it as a hobby, something I enjoy doing in my spare time. With a few free hours on a Sunday afternoon I can scan a handful of pictures and import them into my database. It is light work that I can pick up and put down when I want to. Oskar's journal, however, was an entirely different matter. That was certainly not light work. To tackle that project I would have to learn a new alphabet, read through over a hundred pages of text, translate it, and write it all down. That one was better off on the shelf. Who has that kind of time? I certainly did not.

In the fall of 2012 I was offered a consulting assignment in Manhattan. Living in northwestern New Jersey a trip to Manhattan and back every day is a job in and of itself. First there is the twenty minute drive to the train station and from there it is an hour and a half of sitting on a train. I took the assignment, but dreaded the commute. I was never one to sit still for such a long period of time without accomplishing something. What was I going to do on this long trip? I could take a nap or read a book as do all of the other commuters around me, but what would that accomplish?

Then I remembered the one book I had always wanted to read but never had the time for it. It occurred to me that I could turn that trip into an asset. The job offered me the opportunity that had eluded me for over twenty years. I researched samples of various German handwriting styles and made scans of the pages from Oskar's journal. One letter at a time I pieced together each word. It was difficult and tedious work. Was that a "J"? No. An "F"? Maybe. Perhaps the next letter will help me. This continued one word at a time. It took me an entire week to get through the first page. Some words tripped me up as I discovered that Oskar was not a good speller. I also ran into grammatical errors from time to time which further complicated the effort.

Eventually I made it through the first page and after that week I got better at reading his handwriting. Soon I could do a page in a day, then two pages. I had the journal scan open on my laptop and a new document open in another window. I took the document, arranged it landscape, and cut the page into two columns. I would read a sentence from the journal, switch to the document, write the German on the left side and the English translation in the right column. Then it was on to the next sentence to repeat the process. I was finally on my way to completing this body of work.

I looked forward to that commute each morning so that I may continue the excitement of finding out what happened to him next. The ride to work and back was by far the best part of the day. It was more than a matter of just reading the story, for I could not simply read it. I had to work at it and unpack the experience one word at a time. When I finished, I believed that I had found something much more than a valuable piece of my family's history. It was a time capsule, an original account of World War II from a German soldier never before shared. It described some of the battles of the Eastern Front, the conditions of the Russian military prisons, and the post war struggles of the German families of Lower Silesia displaced by the new Polish government. It's a story that I felt compelled to share, to join the chorus which composes the entire body of experiences from the War.

Along the way I solicited the help of a few colleagues who could translate some of the Russian language that Oskar peppered his story with. One colleague shared that she was born in the Ukrainian city of Dnipropetrovs'k where some parts of the story take place. I wanted to learn if any of the locations were familiar to her. During our conversations, she told me of her own family's struggles during the War as they fled the city along with so many other Jews to take refuge in places like Irkutsk and Uzbekistan. It fascinates me to know that there are millions of people alive today who have amazing stories to tell from that time; stories of bravery, hardship, perseverance, and profound loss. Each is like a star in the sky, dazzling and beautiful in its own right, and at the same time one in an innumerable collection vying for our attention.

I will also take this opportunity to identify others who have provided inspiration, guidance and assistance. I am grateful to Oskar and the help he received to record his experiences so well and preserve them for future generations. I thank my mother for saving Oskar's journal and bringing it back for me to enjoy. Most of all I want to thank my wife, Lisa, and sons David and Jared. I am in awe of their creative talents. They are brilliant, imaginative, articulate, and funny. Lisa was an English major in college. David is an artist and a writer. Jared is just entering high school but is becoming a great storyteller, full of color, character, and imagination. By contrast I studied mathematics in school and work in the technology field. In that respect I may just be their creative opposite. I am thankful to them for showing me a level of artistic talent that provided so much encouragement for this project.

This record of my great uncle's experiences will enhance our understanding of events and conditions on the Eastern Front in World War II. Most of all I hope this story inspires you to renew your interest in your own family's history. Listen to the stories. Write them down. Don't allow them to be lost and forgotten. Share them with your children, nieces, nephews, and cousins. Afford them the opportunity to enrich their lives. The face on that old photograph from the shoebox isn't just an old relative you barely knew as a child. There are a hundred years of experiences behind that face. If you look closely, you will see the gratitude when you take the time to remember.

Chapter 1 MARCHING ORDERS

The date is February tenth, 1946. I've spent the past few months in hiding. The last rays of light from the winter sun shine through a small window, allowing me to examine the narrow space that offers me shelter from the cold wind and prying eyes. There are boxes piled high in every corner, leaving me just enough room on the floor to lie down and stretch my legs. My stomach has been empty so long that it no longer growls for attention, but I still wish that I had something to fill it. I know that I need to get some sleep, but I can't keep my mind away from my wife and my boy. I tell myself that they're safe so long as they keep their distance from me. I'm on the other side of town, a place called Bad Kudowa just over the border from Czechoslovakia. I'm far enough away from them, but close enough to allow me to bring over some food from time to time as I am able to procure any. I go there unseen by cover of night and leave quickly. My parents once lived nearby in a beautiful house here in Bad Kudowa on the edge of a great forest. They will not be coming back to it any time soon, and neither will I.

Tonight I am fortunate to have a roof over my head, in a house that I hope no one will notice. I'm grateful to the woman upstairs for allowing me to stay here. She doesn't know who I am and I don't know her either. In fact, I don't even recall her name. During the day I try to make myself useful by helping around the house or working in the garden.

Some days I'm lucky and find some work that will pay me a few zloty. I give the owner of the house what I can and the rest goes to pay for food, what little there is available to buy. Most days I don't have anything to do except to stay hidden and alert.

My life has changed so much over the last few years. I have spent a great deal of time and effort staying hidden and unknown, but I want people to know who I am and what I've done. I've had an incredible adventure, and it is a story worth telling. The woman has given me an empty notebook and a pen. I still have an hour or two of daylight and I'm not going anywhere this day.

It all started for me in the early hours on the morning of June twenty-second, 1941. I was in the German army's fifth company from Division 298, second battalion, TR525. We had been camped on the Bug River in the town of Hrubieszów for the past few weeks. It was a large fighting force, and we all knew why we were there. The Russians knew it, too. They were stationed on the other side of the river keeping an eye on us. At four o'clock in the morning I was jarred awake by movement in our tent. The men were saying that our commanding officer has summoned our division to meet in the clearing where we had been conducting our training. We proceeded there in an orderly fashion. It was very quiet for such a large group, partly for the fatigue of being jolted out of bed at such an early hour, but mostly in anticipation of what we expected to be the news we had been waiting for.

The commanding officer walked into the middle of the group and announced that the time had come to move east into Russian territory. I had waited anxiously for this day, as we all had, but hearing those words gave me pause. I glanced at the soldier next to me, but he kept his focus on our CO. His face was expressionless, but I knew what he was thinking. We had a lot of hard work ahead of us. Russia is vast and its army huge, but we were confident and ready to get started.

Our division quickly mobilized for battle. Our training and experience were evident as we methodically prepared the equipment and moved into position. Soon the order came and the first explosions ripped through the stillness of the early dawn hours. I stood motionless, staring out to the east in the direction where our cannons were aimed. The wheels were set in motion for an adventure from which there was no turning back. The shelling continued for about half an hour. We hardly spoke at all during this time. When the guns fell silent there was just enough of a pause to hear the order to begin our charge.

We stormed across the Bug toward the city of Ustyluh on the eastern shore of the river. The Russian army was stationed there, the target of our assault. We moved quickly through the fields toward the enemy encampment and announced our arrival with a shower of bullets. Our pace quickened as the resistance we expected never materialized. We found no Russian artillery set up to counter our assault and few defensive positions. Large numbers of Russian soldiers fled their encampment still in their underwear. Many were gunned down as they ran, still more quickly surrendered.

The artillery strike proved to be very effective as we captured the city without much of a fight. The battle was quickly over and I was proud that we had executed our plan so well. My division took our first captives and I accompanied my battalion mates as we led the prisoners back over the Bug to a refugee camp that we erected in anticipation of our success. As we approached the river a group of Russians soldiers taking cover in a wooded area fired upon us for the first time. Although the skirmish ended quickly my company suffered its first fatalities of the war. Fortunately we were able to rescue six wounded soldiers after the brief counter-attack and bring them back to the safety of our camp on the eastern side of the Bug, near the town of Hrubieszów.

Our division regrouped in Hrubieszów but we would not stay there long. We readied our equipment, turned around and headed back across the River, pushing further into Russian territory. The next town in our path, just a few kilometers east of Ustyluh, was Volodymyr-Volynskyi. Our assault also began with a barrage of heavy artillery before charging into the town. We suffered a greater number of casualties that day as the Russians were now not so easily caught by surprise. Though the numbers of dead and wounded started to rise, we still captured the town without much of a struggle. The war had started well but we knew that a much greater challenge stood before us, namely the Ukrainian capital city of Kiev. That deed would require a much larger fighting force.

It was a long march eastward to Kiev. We met little resistance along the way as the Russian forces quickly gave up ground to form a defensive line at Kiev. We reached the outskirts of the city and for the next six days we prepared for the battle to come. Just before the orders came in to attack the city, we received reinforcements to replace our dead and wounded soldiers, as well as additional weapons and ammunition. The German forces formed a ring around the capitol to cut off the Russian troops inside the city and close it in for the battle.

My division began its attack from the north of Kiev through the town of Boryspil. Once Kiev was surrounded, we softened their defenses with a sustained artillery barrage then charged into the city. The division commander identified the radio station as an important early target, and it was our battalion that was called upon to carry out the order to seize the facility. We were successful and secured the station. It wasn't long before the German forces prevailed as the city defenses fell. Kiev was ours.

In August, the division received new marching orders to head out from Kiev toward the city of Poltava. Before doing so, our company took a five day break from fighting to regroup. At this time the commander released our casualty reports and the numbers were very high. We lost six corporals, one sergeant, and eighteen field soldiers. There was also a small number of wounded. The size of our company shrank from one hundred and eighty to one hundred and twenty-three men. The division commander shared the casualty reports with the entire 298th division. He mentioned in the report that the division will need replacement for some of the people and equipment. The last words in the report were "When the division has recovered, it will be time to move on." We knew not to get too comfortable here.

The five day break we enjoyed after our victory in Kiev was over too quickly. New instructions arrived ordering us to instead march onto the town of Balakliia, which lies one hundred and twenty kilometers southeast from the city of Kharkiv on the river Donets. Along the way we stopped and made camp in the village of Chuhuiv, also on the Donets. We held that position from December eleventh to December twelfth, 1941. This would be our fallback point if we needed it. On December twelfth we again received new instructions to march instead on the town of Izyum, which was south of Balakliia along the Donets River. We left immediately. A few days later we entered Izyum to find that Russians troops had been there before us, but had since left. It was evident that the Russians had thoroughly sacked the city. Meeting with no resistance, we paused to make camp here during the Christmas holiday.

On December twenty-fourth during our Christmas celebration, the sound of bells was drowned out by the explosions of artillery fire. The Russians tried to catch us off-guard and break through our position. They bombarded the city throughout the entire night, but they could not wrest us from our position. Our defense of the city held and the Russians eventually withdrew.

On December twenty-eighth the third battalion swapped out the second battalion and afforded us a break from the fighting. The third battalion remained in Izyum to hold the city, while we were allowed to retreat further east into German-held territory and regroup. We marched along the river a few kilometers west to the village of Petrivs'ke, where we would set up camp for a brief rest. Above all else, what we wanted was to get cleaned up. We were filthy and so were our uniforms. Throughout our recent encampments and encounters with the enemy we suffered terribly from being covered with lice. No matter where you reached out with your hand, you can clench your fist and grab several of them. Unfortunately for us, no sooner had we set out our belongings to get cleaned, we were ordered to pack everything back up and get back on the move.

The Russians were threatening to break through our defenses in Izyum. Our battalion headed west, away from the city. By January 13, 1942 the Russians gathered a great mass of soldiers and tanks just outside of town. They stormed through our firing positions, their tanks rolling right over the gun barrels of our artillery. We did not have the forces to hold them back and so we surrendered Izyum to the Russians and withdrew. It marked our first retreat of the war as our forces fled back over the Donets River.

We turned south to make our retreat through Barvinkove to the city of Pavlograd. The last encounter with the Russian army was a rough one and left the entire division on edge. The commanders set up a gathering point in the city center for the 298th division and the harried soldiers raced into the square to their designated positions. We were ordered into groups by company and battalion. Whatever break we had from fighting was brief. Before we knew it, we turned around and marched twenty kilometers back toward Barvinkove at what was now the front line.

As we reformed the front line in Barvinkove, we were surprised to learn that the second battalion was joined by a Romanian division. We laughed to ourselves when we saw them approach. The caps they wore made them look ridiculous. Still, they were on our side, so we tried to work with them as well as we could.

Our battalion commander's name was Kurt Schille. He was well-respected by the men under his command as a brave leader and good strategist. He also had a decorated past. In September 1939 he was a corporal during the campaign in Poland. There he demonstrated strong tactical knowledge and leadership. He was called back to Berlin in 1942 where he received the Knight's Cross with Oak Leaves and promoted to captain. We were honored to have him with us.

Once again our assignments were shuffled around. The second battalion was pulled back out of the Romanian division and replaced by another, older division. We received new reinforcements, increasing the size of our company from forty-one to one hundred and twenty men. We were now ready for action.

Our new instructions were to provide cover for our scouting patrols, as they crossed the front line into Russian-controlled territory to bring back recognizance information. They were sent to observe Russian troop movement in the interior and to determine if new troops were coming over the Donets River. In the meantime, we knew that a German tank group pushed down on the city of Kharkiv from the north and another up from the south. We were beginning to form a circle around Kharkiv, cutting it off from Russian reinforcements.

The blockade around Kharkiv was completed on May 15, 1942. Our combat sector remained very quiet, as was the entire 525 regiment in a Romanian sector stationed to the right of us. We oriented our position with that of the Romanian position and began to build massive bunkers. The bunkers were laid out in groups according to directions from the regional commander who inspected our work. The bunkers had to be three meters by five meters and two point eight meters deep. They were covered with railroad ties that we tore up from tracks that ran through the area. The railroad ties were laid in a cross over the bunker, from which two people could shoot. The floor was built up ninety centimeters, also out of railroad ties.

The bunkers needed to be graded well to avoid being detected by the enemy. The entrance to the bunkers faced away from the front line. We started digging the trenches by hand using railroad picks but the ground was so hard that you could only break off a few kilos of soil at a time. We labored long and hard on the task with little progress to show for our hard work, but our pace never slowed. The battalion commander strode back and forth along the trenches we were digging and reminded us what every good soldier from the Eastern lands was taught: "Every resistance can be broken." Eventually we adopted a new approach. We dug holes thirty centimeters in circumference. We gathered six hand grenades, bound them together, and shoved them into the hole. Then we made a fuse ten meters long. Three seconds after we lit the fuse, the charges were detonated and the ground was loosened up. The men couldn't wait to dive right into the dirt. Shovels and picks were flying as the trenches grew deep.

Meter by meter we dug deeper into the earth and constructed our fortification. On May nineteenth, 1942 as we finished the bunkers, we were joined by the Romanian segment. Together we began the assault on Kharkiv on May twentieth. At five o'clock in the morning, we prepared the Romanian artillery. It had proven itself well in the Russian campaign and earned our respect. On the other hand, the infantry of the Romanian army was completely useless. Everyone knows that the Romanians are nothing more than a nation of gypsies and bastard children. The artillery fired on the town for a half an hour. Around six thirty the bombardment ceased. I climbed out of the bunker to get a good starting position and laid flat on the ground waiting for the signal. When it came, I got to my feet quickly to join a wave of German and Romanian forces charging across the open fields toward the city. At first we shouted at our enemy, but after a few hundred meters of running we could see that the edge of town was still almost two kilometers away. As we neared our target, the bullets fired from the city defenders whistled passed our ears. Grenade fragments lashed against our cheeks. Still we ran across the fields, undeterred and unafraid. My target was still four kilometers away in the city center. It was a long and dangerous run through enemy fire, but I made it into the city with my battalion. I reached a two-story building and ducked for cover to catch my breath. Several of my comrades joined me. I put my head down and saw that the elbow of my left sleeve was soaked with blood. Undeterred, I readied my weapon, looked around at the men from my battalion, and gave the signal to continue on, into the streets.

The battle lasted for about seven hours before our opponent's guns fell quiet. Our forces prevailed and the town was captured.

Almost immediately, we braced ourselves for a counterattack from our opponent. We took up defensive positions in the city and waited, but no counterattack came. This allowed our paramedics to clear the dead and wounded from the battlefield. My own company's losses were light. We had four dead and eleven wounded. Out of the wounded, five were severe and six were minor. Two of those slightly wounded stayed with the troops.

Later that afternoon the stillness was broken. Blue smoke appeared to the left of the first battalion. That meant that tanks were approaching for an attack. The first battalion dropped back two kilometers towards the front line to form an angle, shielding the defensive line to prevent further losses during the engagement. Our battalion commander was wise. He embedded himself in the foremost line and gave us the order to keep still and allow the Russian tanks to advance further. When the Russians had reached our target zone the Romanian artillery fired a barrage on the oncoming vehicles. Immediately we set five of them ablaze. The others turned and fled. That was the last we had heard from the Russians for a while.

The next morning on the twenty-first of May the Romanian cavalry readied itself for a new offensive. They left the post at five o'clock for the city of Lozova. The Romanians would attack from the south and we would attack from the north to take the city. We made swift work of the battle. On May twenty-second around six o'clock in the evening, the city of Lozova fell into German hands for the second time.

Chapter 2   THE TRENCHES OF PETRIVS'KE

We stayed in Lozova and finally got a day of rest. On the next day, our division left Lozova and marched along the Donets toward Izyum. On the twenty-seventh of May, 1942 we approached the town of Petrivs'ke, which was still held by Russian forces. They staunchly defended their position, but the ring we made around the town closed tightly around them. We put up a strong effort and hit the town hard, but we were not able to penetrate their defenses. We needed help.

The German Luftwaffe was called in support of the troops. As soon as the aircraft were inserted into the attack, the advantage turned in our favor. One by one every target was hit. During the entire campaign, I have never witnessed such an awesome display of force. The Russians knew they were outmatched and tried to flee, but every tank, cavalry, and infantryman that attempted to escape the enclosure was bombed.

It was a victory, yes, but one that was difficult for me to celebrate as we watched the town of Petrivs'ke go up in flames. The Russian forces defending the town were decimated. There were fifteen hundred inhabitants and it was hard to imagine that many of them survived.

As we moved into the burning village, the battalion commander gave our company instructions to clear a trench that ran from the west of Petrivs'ke out to the north along a two kilometer row of trees. Our mission was not complete until we had cleared out all enemy forces. First Lieutenant Scheg called together his platoon and group leaders to assess the situation. It was ten o'clock in the morning when we received our orders and began our sweep of the area. As we approached the two kilometer long trench, the area looked familiar to me. It was the same path that we had taken on our retreat from Izyum a few months ago. I made my commander aware of this. We reached the trench at the edge of town by eleven o'clock that morning. We were met there by a German panzer and its crew. They had taken prisoners and asked us for help. I told my commander that I would take two of the Russian prisoners with me under my protection. He nodded in agreement.

I assumed control of the first platoon while the commander took the second. I took the two Russians and made them walk in front of me, hands over their head where I could keep my eye on them. My platoon marched behind me. We were separated from my commander and his platoon, as he passed over the trench while I went through it. We trekked carefully through the first one hundred meters of the trench when we met our first Russian soldier who had been hiding out there. He immediately raised his hands and threw down his weapon. I sent him back into the platoon that was following behind. As we continued through the trench I came upon more Russian soldiers. They, too, surrendered without incident.

The trench was very deep, and full of twists, turns, and dark corners. I eventually lost contact with my commander and the platoon above me. My comrades following in the trench behind me fell out of sight from time to time, while I walked ahead with my two captives that I took from the tank crew. I turned a corner and came upon a hideout. A Russian combatant lay on the ground four meters in front. He had a gunshot wound in the knee. I called out to him in Russian "Are you armed?" sounding each word clearly and forcefully. He answered "No." With my eyes still trained on my two captives, I approached him and I pulled him up off the ground. I checked him for weapons, and finding none sent him back to my platoon. Then I heard whispers coming from the hideout. I crept closer, listening carefully for any sound that may signal trouble. There was a cover through which a hole had been dug out. I saw a hint of movement from the small amount of light that penetrated the darkness behind the door.

I shouted in Russian "Come out of there right now!" A set of fingers emerged between the boards covering the dugout and pushed them aside. Three men climbed out, a first lieutenant and two soldiers. They still had their weapons with them, but they all laid them to the ground and threw up their hands immediately. I heard a shaky voice utter "Please do not shoot."

"Do not be afraid" I answered. "No harm will come to you if you cooperate." I lowered the barrel of the submachine-gun and moved in to disarm the men. As I took my first step closer, I paid the price for letting down my guard. It was a single gunshot. The bullet struck me in the upper part of my right thigh. It pierced me all the way through, coming out of my buttocks. It felt as though I had been struck with a hammer. Then my leg became stiff. I let out a howl as I tumbled to the ground, hitting the soft dirt with a thud. I quickly propped myself up and trained my gun on them. I clenched my teeth to push back the pain. I glared at the men with my finger on the trigger, scanning them for any provocative action that offered me an excuse to fire back at them. They all had a look of surprise on their face, as if they didn't understand what had just happened. They also knew their own lives were now at risk, staring down, unarmed, at a wounded enemy combatant with a gun pointed at them.

My comrades behind me heard the shot and my scream. They raced through the winding trench up to my position. As they approached, I saw one of them try to escape. It was a fourth Russian combatant, one I failed to notice at first. He was a commissar who hid behind the Russian First Lieutenant and the two soldiers that I had seen emerge from the hideout. While the other three raised their weapons to surrender, this soldier held on to his pistol, stretched it out between the men, and fired the shot that struck me. As I watched him start to make his way down the trench, I calmly gave the trigger of my submachine-gun one press. The commissar fell to the ground. At that moment, my platoon reached me. Some of my men ran ahead to the fallen Russian soldier and fired a few more shots into him out of anger.

The three Russian soldiers were searched and taken back with the others that we had captured. My comrades helped me up and carried me through the rest of the trench to complete our mission. One of them climbed out of the trench to bring the news to the company leader of the other platoon, patrolling the area above, to inform him of the shooting. A short time later the two platoons met up at the end of the trench. It was coming up on twelve thirty. We called for the medics and our group was the first to be received by them.

One of the doctors gave me a quick examination. He turned to the company leader and uttered to him that they needed to get me into the village right away because of the possibility that my main artery was hit. The leader took control over the entire company and gave the order to pull back. We carried out his orders and turned to head toward the village. We had captured a total of sixty-eight prisoners. There was one vehicle and a pair of horses waiting to cart the wounded. I was carried out on the vehicle with four other wounded Russian prisoners. My platoon climbed back into the trench to make one more sweep, before returned to our camp in the town center.

As the transport started toward the village, we encountered six Russian double-deckers in our path. It was clear they had witnessed the whole affair, and we immediately we took on fire. One of the wounded Russians lying next to me found the gate to the back of the truck. He managed to open it and roll out of the moving vehicle to the ground. Some of our troops stayed behind to battle the Russian forces that remained in the area while the rest of our company and the truck that carried me hurried back into the center of Petrivs'ke.

Once we reached the town, I was rushed to the medic who attended to me right away. His examination determined that the artery was not hit. The bullet had missed it by only two centimeters. It also just missed hitting my lymph nodes. I was relieved to learn that I would be okay. He gave me an injection to guard against infection. That would tide me over until I could receive more comprehensive treatment. I was put back on the transport and taken to the main headquarters our forces had set up in town. I needed to stay there overnight because it was not safe to fly out and there was still the danger of encountering more artillery fire.

Few houses in town survived the siege. Our forces moved in to occupy those that still stood, setting up command centers and places for the troops to rest. The available space was filled very quickly. With no room in any of the remaining houses, the medics moved me into a barn along with the rest of the injured. There were twelve other German soldiers among the wounded and a number of Russian captives. I tried to get some rest, but it wasn't long before the evening silence was broken by the sounds of battle. That night at around midnight, the Russian cavalry tried to fight its way back into Petrivs'ke. The position was important to the Russians because they had set up a regional command center there.

We were all lying together in the barn on makeshift beds, listening to the sounds of the fighting that was waging around us. We were, of course, unable to affect the outcome, but some of the wounded soldiers didn't see it that way. The Russians cheered on the advancing Kazaks with shouts of "hurray, hurray!" Even the German wounded felt compelled to lend their support to our side with their own shouts of encouragement. I found the courage they exhibited to be quite comical because we had no protection at all and also no weapons by us. The thought crossed my mind if the Russians were to burst in here we had no way to defend ourselves.

Our opponent had a rough time of it and felt the force of the German weaponry we had moved in. They suffered heavy casualties in their attempt to take back the town. The battle lasted for an hour and a half before the Russians abandoned the siege and retreated. The sound of explosions and gunfire quickly dwindled before ceasing altogether. My wounded comrades also stopped their shouting and I could finally get some rest.

A few hours later, around four o'clock the next morning, the medics showed up and carried us one by one onto the bed of a truck. We were laid out ten men across. I was grouped with all of the wounded soldiers who needed to be transported lying down. We traveled thirty kilometers to an emergency airfield in Barvinkove. There stood seven Junker JU88 airplanes onto which we were loaded, and at seven o'clock in the morning the planes took off and we were flown to Dnipropetrovs'k.

After we landed, we were carried off the plane into a large hanger for processing. What we saw was gruesome sight and made us fearful and uneasy. Laid out on stretchers across the entire hanger as far as we could see were injured German soldiers. There were so many of them, horribly wounded and suffering. Most of the casualties were from the Battle of Kharkiv, which ended on May twenty-ninth, 1942. I waited there for some time before it was my turn to be processed. After a quick examination, I was taken into an ambulance and driven to a military hospital in the nearby town of Nowomoskowsk. I stayed there for nine days.

On June eighth I was back on the move. I boarded a medical transport train that brought me to the city of Lemberg in Poland. We stayed in Lemberg for five days. From there it was on through Poland, across Czechoslovakia, and then into Saxony. My final destination was the town of Arnsdorf near the city of Dresden. I stayed in Arnsdorf until the doctors declared that I was completely recovered. I was lucky with my wound, because the shot went clean through and it was healing well. I knew that I would soon be back at the Front Line.

Chapter 3   RE-CAPTURE THE HIGHLAND

On August twentieth the doctors released me from the military hospital. The army assigned me to replacement troop division number 164, stationed in Metz in the Elsass-Lothringen region. I reported to the division on August twenty-fourth and was immediately given three weeks of recovery time off, plus an additional two weeks of vacation at home.

My vacation ended on the twelfth of October, 1942. I left the replacement division and was next assigned to a field battalion at Baumholder, a training facility near Saarbrucken. It was odd to call it a training facility, as there were no weapons provided to us. I assumed it was because they were being conserved for the fighting. Two days after arriving at Baumholder they did furnish me with a new uniform. The battalion was overstaffed at the time, so they sent the youngest soldiers, mostly nineteen year olds, to join the replacement troops in Metz. We didn't stay in Baumholder long, as on the fourth of December it was back to the Eastern Front in Russia. The trip was interrupted with a four-day stay over in Rengersdorf near the city of Glatz. On December twelfth our trip resumed and I found myself once again in that paradise which was the Soviet territory.

The trip took us over Lemberg and through Dnipropetrovs'k toward the city of Stalino. From there we

traveled to Horlivka, then on to Voroshilovgrad and finally
to Kamensk-Shakhtinsky. We spent our Christmas holiday
en route. Our marching orders took us back to my old unit,
which by that time had found itself in Donbogen near
Kamensk. However we could not yet rejoin my division as
it was closed in by Russian forces and inaccessible, so we
stayed in Kamensk until it was safe to meet up with them.

Kamensk was bustling with activity. Throughout
the city there were several troop details that were returning
from the front line in Stalingrad and others that had come out
of Caucasus region. Many of the troops were brought back
to assemble in Kamensk in order to rebuild the front line
there and resist the advancing Russian army. Unfortunately
for us, the enemy now had superior numbers and we could
no longer hold them back. It wasn't long before our ground
troops were ordered to retreat toward Voroshilovgrad. When
we got to within thirty kilometers of Voroshilovgrad, we
encountered the 304th division from Saxony, who was in
retreat from its position on the Donets River in Luhansk. As
we got within sight we displayed our weapons to each other,
holding them high over our heads in a silent, solemn solute.
A few steps later we were dutifully on our separate ways.

While in Kamensk I was reassigned again, this time
to the 574th regiment, sixth company, second battalion. It
was with that unit where I would again be thrown into
combat. The men in the regiment had very little battle
experience and had yet to encounter the Russians. The
division was stationed for two years in France, but because
the large Russian territory required more troops, they were
relocated to fight the east. The regiment commander Oberst
sensed that the troops were uneasy and assembled the
division to speak directly with them. He told us that the

division will be in service until April first, 1943. He ended his address with stern encouragement: "Soldiers," he said, "you are tested and accomplished fighters, and I see in every one of you a distinction that you will earn in the East."

The second battalion of this company held the same number of troops as in my old unit, company six. We had a complement of sixty men, but when I got there this new company did not have a leader. Eventually we did get one and he joined the company for the first time as we were about to march out. Shortly after he arrived, the battalion commander assembled all of the group and platoon leaders. He told us that early tomorrow morning at three o'clock we have an important military target. We need to recapture a highland area that the Germans once held. These heights had already cost us many lives. It was for us, as well as for our opponent, a very valuable and strategic position.

We were on the western side of the Donets. Our mission was to capture and hold a stretch of land on a hill, which was also on the western side of the river. There was a small town situated two kilometers behind the hills on our side. Beyond that, there was an enemy camp heavily fortified with grenadiers. They needed to be taken out before we could advance on the heights. The plan was to get past the Russian defensive forces and move our weapons and vehicles through the town and into position to capture the highlands. If the Russians wanted to hold that position, they would need to destroy the vehicles and artillery we moved there.

My battalion's orders were to maneuver past the town and around the highlands, to observe and engage our opponent, when and if he tried to bring more troops or equipment across the water to reinforce his position in the hills. The battalion commander repeated to us often that early morning at two o'clock we needed to be at our departure position. Then he left, bestowing upon us the best of luck for the soldiers. The company leader made it clear that tomorrow morning at three o'clock the battle would begin.

In the evening around ten o'clock, our company made its way back into Kamensk where the battalion kept its fighting units. We had to march through the village in deep snow. By two o'clock we arrived in the town. We spent two long hours warming ourselves in the houses we occupied. Then the dispatcher brought the order to be at the departure point in an hour. We packed up and assembled at the departure point where we prepared to move out. The battalion commander was visibly nervous, and it was amusing to see him scurry back and forth around the troops. He ordered the company to move to the right, then to the left, then back to the right. Throughout this layover, our opponent took notice and became aware of the activity.

The commander warned us that we would be facing heavy weaponry, including two assault guns, artillery, and heavily armed grenadiers. However the soldiers looked battle-ready, and paid no mind to the warnings. We were anxious to get started, as the original plan was to strike at our target at three o'clock and it was now almost six o'clock.

Just after he gave us the warning, we began to experience the heavy weaponry that the commanders in Berlin told us were there. At six o'clock, the orders to march came in for the battalion that was now one hundred and sixty men strong, including our company that was the largest with sixty men. Our company had very few veteran soldiers and only one experienced leader. That would soon change.

We were two hundred meters along on the battlefield, when suddenly we saw the armed attack coming from the right. This caught us off guard, as we had prepared for an attack from the left side. We had moved our heavy weaponry into position for an assault on the left and worked hard to keep our assets hidden from sight. We were tricked into thinking that was where the Russians had set up their camp. It was a ruse, a dummy camp, and we fell for it. There was no one there.

That whole wing had to pivot to target the heavy weaponry of our opponent. Stalin's artillery and heavily-armed grenadiers were firing at us from an encampment in the woods on the other side, on the banks of the Donets. Fortunately we reacted quickly and executed the change in tactics exceedingly well. We fired back, hitting them hard. The battle was a success, and we accomplished our mission of forcing our opponents out of their position and captured the highland area for ourselves. It was just a small, three hundred meter strip of land, but it held plenty of military assets that were now ours, including eight heavy machine guns, three bazookas, a number of rifles, and thirty-eight prisoners. The rest of the enemy troops fled back over the Donets.

During the battle our battalion commander was nowhere to be seen. As we finished occupying the position he suddenly appeared. I was with him when he proudly notified the regional commander "mission accomplished". He relayed how many weapons he seized, the number of prisoners, and that the rest of the defeated troops were chased over the Donets. The regional commander asked him how high our losses were, but he didn't answer because he had not yet been briefed on that.

We learned that the losses in our company were in fact very high. Out of a complement of sixty men we had forty-three casualties. The company's first lieutenant Ramm was also killed. While we accomplished the mission, our situation was tenable. Only seventeen men were left to defend the land, but we knew that we needed at least sixty people to do so. By ten o'clock the Russians had quieted down and the dead could now be cleared from the battlefield. I received my third wound in this battle, but I had no interest in another recovery vacation and wanted to stay with the troops.

At eleven o'clock, the battalion commander met with me for a second time. He came into my tent and asked me what the situation is. I told him what had taken place and that I maneuvered trucks around our position to fortify our defense in preparation for a counter attack. The battalion commander took note of my name, probably for a commendation similar to the one I received a year ago. He said that he needed me to hold everyone together while he sought reinforcements. He left at once for the regiment headquarters which was six kilometers behind us. He gave me an exact time, it was 11:15, and said that in one hour reinforcements will arrive. He promised me that when the reinforcements came, that I could leave the area with my sixteen men. Somehow I did not find that very reassuring. I told him that it was not safe here, and if the reinforcements do not arrive by three o'clock in the afternoon that I will pull all the men out.

By three o'clock the reinforcements had not yet arrived. I sent one of my comrades into a fox hole to keep a watch for the enemy and alert us with a red flare if they started to advance on us. At a quarter past three, I gave the sign for my comrade to leave the fox hole. We could no longer wait for reinforcements; it was time to abandon our position that we sacrificed so much to capture. I made my way toward the village that we came through the night before. I learned that a supply chain with reinforcements did attempt to come through, but they turned around and retreated to the fall-back position when they encountered enemy forces. They were also bringing the wounded back. We were only one hundred meters from the town, when suddenly there appeared a flare. That was a sign for us that the Russians had moved in to occupy the village. The supply train with their wounded was captured and now in Russian hands.

I had to find another way back. I took out a compass and map and led my men around the town and back to the regiment command post. By the time I got there it was twelve o'clock midnight. I reported to the regional commander and informed him of the situation. He seemed to be aware of it already. He asked me about the strength of our company. I answered – sixteen men. The regional commander was interested in my name, and I was proud to tell him.

I found a house where my comrades and I could rest. We waited there for more orders that would tell us what would happen to us and the rest of our company. It was now January twenty-seventh, 1943. We ended up spending quite some time in the village. I took the opportunity to see a doctor in order to treat the wound I received during the battle. It was a back injury caused by grenade shrapnel, and it was starting to get a little painful. The medic gave me an injection against tetanus. As the wound was not severe I was declared ready for combat. After a while the pain in my back started to go away and it gave me no more trouble.

After seeing the doctor, I headed back to join my company and found the battalion commander waiting for me. Along the way I observed very lively troop movements, particularly anti-tank weapons. The battalion commander gave us notice that at five o'clock we would begin a new attack with support from this equipment. Five additional assault weapons would join the attack later. Looking past the town there was that large hill. That was again the target, and our battalion stood ready to attack.

The battle started punctually at five o'clock. We heard the clash of the assault guns as the explosions rolled across the enemy camp. The shelling went on for half an hour before the enemy abandoned the hill. We moved our forces in to re-take the position. This time there was very little left behind by the Russians, only 3 SMG's and a small number of riffles. The losses on our side were slight. Aside from experiencing a few malfunctions of our assault cannons, everything went according to plan. As our forces moved onto the hill, the entire front quieted down. A First Lieutenant from Company Eight took control over the camp. The mechanized infantry and assault weapons pulled back into town. I stayed with the rest of my company and climbed into an observation post. When I got there, I looked down and saw that in front of the post there lay three fallen comrades, all stripped naked for their clothing and belongings.

It wasn't long before the calm was broken by a faint but disturbing sound. Every five minutes my comrades stationed in the camp would approach me and say they hear the sound of chain saws and falling tree trunks. We concluded that the Russians were cutting down the trees to build a bridge over the Donets to allow their tanks to cross. We brought this to the attention of the battalion commander. He hurried right out to the observation post. He heard the noise for himself, but wouldn't draw any conclusions. He repeated to us over and over that we must hold and defend our position. He then returned to his command post. His last words were to let him know if anything out of the ordinary happens.

At five o'clock in the morning we saw in the distance the silhouettes of Russian vehicles that were collecting and transporting casualties from the battlefield. By five thirty the Russian activity picked up. Suddenly something out of the ordinary did happen. A Russian vehicle appeared just one hundred and fifty meters from us. It was equipped with a loudspeaker, and a voice called out: "Comrades, come out. We will give you a vacation. We will give you a Führer Package." We replied with a volley of bullets. They ran for cover, but after a few minutes they returned and repeated their announcements on the loudspeaker. For the second time we gave them another volley. We exchanged gunfire but it didn't last long and the Russian troops retreated.

After that we heard the sound of chains again, and this time it grew louder. Their tanks were on the move. We had a very weak position as we were short on men. We waited for an attack, but the Russian infantry did not advance right away as they were probably waiting for the support from their tanks.

Someone remarked that we had not seen our commander in a while. We wondered aloud if the Russians had captured the first lieutenant during this skirmish. The eighth company returned to the command post and informed us that the officer had taken a bullet to the head during the recent exchange. He was dead. We waited there while the sound of the chainsaws was getting closer.

It wasn't long before the first two tank turrets were in sight. I warned the battalion that two tanks were headed toward the command post and were about three hundred meters away. The commander told me to hold still, as he could not see any. I contacted him again, telling him that there were now ten new tanks joining the attack. Then he was able to see the first two tanks just two hundred meters from the command post. The battalion commander knew that our position was untenable and he gave us the orders to leave and save ourselves if we can. The whole regiment knew we would not be able to withstand such an assault, and ultimately the commander gave the order for everyone to retreat and march toward Voroshilovgrad. There we would re-form the division.

Chapter 4   THE AIR FIELD

We received a reinforcement team at Voroshilovgrad. We made camp north of an airfield and safely held our position there until February fifth.

On the morning of February fifth, Russians forces moved in quickly without warning and began to fire upon us. It wasn't long before they overwhelmed us, chased us away, and took control over the base. We did have a number of anti-tank weapons defending the airfield, but every one of them had seized up and would not function. We retreated to a position safely away from the air base and called for reinforcements from a near-by S.S. regiment to help us take the airfield back from the Russians. They arrived in no time, and we worked together with the S.S. mechanized infantry that was spread out across the battlefield. We easily took back the airfield from the Russians, who only managed to hold it for about five hours.

We moved in quickly to make a clean sweep of the base. I led my battalion to a small house on the grounds. We kicked the door in and charged inside. As we entered, we saw four Russian soldiers run out of the first floor down into the basement. We chased after them and disarmed them without incident. Then we searched the adjacent room and came upon three German comrades from the Luftwaffe; two were bound to chairs, one private and one private first class. The third, a staff sergeant, was lying face down on the floor.

He was barely alive. I was initially startled at the sight of the two bound men. Their hair was white. I had never seen a combat soldier with white hair.

The two men were in shock. We released them from the chairs and tried to talk with them, but they would not say a word. About an hour later they started to recover and they told us what had happened. When the Russians attacked the base, the three men fell into enemy hands. The four Russian soldiers that we captured in the house were responsible for keeping watch over them. The two were quickly bound to the chairs. The staff sergeant broke loose and fought to free the two others but he was subdued. One of the Russians found a piston and beat him over the head with it repeatedly until he collapsed to the ground.

An SS platoon that followed us into the house took the four Russian prisoners and the three men from the Luftwaffe. A doctor that was stationed with the SS troops examined the injured staff sergeant and determined that the Luftwaffe officer would not recover from his injuries. The other two were starting to speak more clearly and told us of their experience. They were transported to a hospital right away. The deceased staff sergeant was taken to a cemetery for the German military in Voroshilovgrad to be laid to rest.

A few days later, the Russians came back with a vengeance and pounded us non-stop. They brought in their own air force and dropped so many bombs on Voroshilovgrad that it was barely recognizable. The German army was forced to pull the troops out from the area south of Voroshilovgrad and from out of the Caucasus region. We feared that we had lost the city.

Chapter 5   RETREAT

We retreated to a position not far away from
Voroshilovgrad. On Saturday, February eleventh, we were
told that when red flares were visible in the sky it was the
sign that we would double back and take the fight to the
enemy. Early morning at three o'clock on February twelfth,
we saw the flares. We left the camp, assembled on the path,
and marched west back towards Voroshilovgrad. This time
we were completely disorganized. There were groups of
soldiers from many different divisions, and we were
confused about what the mission was. As we got closer to
Voroshilovgrad, we saw to our surprise that the Russians had
not moved in forces to defend the city, so we marched right
in. We arrived at a meeting point in the city center and were
instructed to gather in groups of our own divisions. I greeted
two of my comrades at our gathering point, but someone
there handed me orders to return to my original unit.

Our new destination was Kremenchuk, a long
journey of one thousand and sixty kilometers. Sadly for us
the railway connection was broken and we had to figure out
for ourselves the fastest way to get there. We concluded the
only viable option was to go on foot. On February
fourteenth, we started marching out from Voroshilovgrad
through Horlivka, Stalino, Mariupol, Saporischschja,
Dnipropetrovs'k, and finally to Kremenchuk. It was a brutal
trek through the harsh winter weather.

We arrived on March eighth in Kremenchuk and I
met up with my former unit. It was great to be together
again with my old division and company. The division

stayed in Kremenchuk waiting for troop replacements for the soldiers they had lost. They had recently suffered considerable losses. On two occasions they had been surrounded and trapped near the town of Donbogen, but each time they succeeded in breaking through to safety. The second time they moved out into the countryside toward Kremenchuk, and they waited there until they received reinforcements. On April second after receiving reinforcements, the division was declared ready for deployment.

On April fifth we received the order to deploy to the town of Slavyansk. Not long after we arrived, our commanders sent us twenty kilometers east to the village of Oleksandrivka on the Donets. There we relieved a division and took over security of the village. Our forces consisted mainly of scouts and assault troops. The security detail lasted until the twelfth of May, at which time we were replaced by a different regiment, and pulled back nine kilometers without incident. It had been a quiet deployment, evidently too quiet for our commanders. So at four o'clock, they sent us marching again, this time ten kilometers east to the front line. When we arrived, we marched up and back along the line. We were told that the purpose was to create a deception for our opponent, to make him believe there were more troops than there actually were. In reality it looked to me that we were simply one and the same regiment, just aimlessly marching back and forth.

On May eighteenth, it was time once again for my three week vacation. I went back to visit my mother. I was looking forward to seeing her again. It was good to be away from the front line and not to think about it for a while. I arrived home on May twenty-second. I was happy to be home, but in the back of my mind I could find no peace. I couldn't stop thinking that this vacation will soon be over and I'll be headed back to the fighting. We often listened to the news together. It brought new reports that the Russians were threatening us along the Donets. On June thirteenth, my vacation had come to an end. Somehow I had the feeling it would be my last. It was time to head back to the God-forsaken Russian territory.

On June seventeenth, I arrived in Sloviansk, where I found a whole host of problems waiting for me. The Russian forces had reached the edge of town and had set up artillery. We knew they had a clear way in. I looked for my division but couldn't find them. I approached the railway guard and asked him if my division had been moved. I learned that they had taken up a position north of Sloviansk, and I received orders to join them. So I began to walk. I reached the main road that led to Kharkiv where my division was located. Along the way, I passed a newly-erected cemetery for German soldiers. I paused to reflect that during my absence many of my comrades were likely laid to rest there. I soon reached the supply line for the company, and after an hour and a half of walking I met up with my division. There I received instructions, as to where to find my battalion.

At ten o'clock in the evening the cooks were finally able to serve the company a meal, as it was not possible to have one during the day. I took my rations back to my tent and began to lay out my gear. As I ate, I looked around. There were many new faces in the company. Among them was a whole battalion made up of Russian Turks. They were Vlasov troops, immediately recognizable by their slanted eyes. They looked pathetic. They had to be the weakest group of soldiers the German army has ever seen.

Though I unpacked some of my belongings, I was hesitant to get too comfortable. The enemy was so close. Anything could happen. We were all wondering what awaits us over the next few days. Then the sound of Russian fire put us in a completely different mood.

Our post was at the edge of a forest. Our opponent took cover behind a flat area of land just two hundred meters away. The incoming fire from the Russians was intermittent but it went on for day and night. Our opponent would not quiet down, because his goal as we understood it, was to retake the town of Sloviansk by the twenty-fifth of June. We had a feeling that we would not be able to stop the Russians, as we knew the weakness of our forces here. But we did hold them back well beyond the twenty-fifth of June, and took solace that we thwarted their plans to some degree.

One month later the town fell back into enemy hands, but that was only because we pulled our forces out in a planned retreat. The military leaders decided the army would fall back to the town of Dnieper and regroup there. We began our withdrawal on June twenty-fifth. It proceeded very deliberately. We started by destroying every large structure in the town. We tore up all the railway tracks leading into the city. We detonated every train bridge and river crossing. Then the entire population was driven out of the town; every person and every animal. In the end, the whole town was set ablaze. It was a horrific scene. As we made our way out, we heard the screams from the villagers and saw the burned carcasses of the animals. Every silo and every granary was set on fire. We did this to every town, every village in our path. When night fell you could see from many kilometers away the burning villages left behind from the aftermath of our march through Eastern Ukraine. It was a terrible site, and I took no pleasure in it.

The methodical retreat of the German army continued for many months, burning grain and flesh along the way. On September twenty-seventh, we crossed the Dnieper into the town of Dnipropetrovs'k. After the last division made its way over the river, we detonated all of the bridges. We immediately set up a new camp on the banks of the Dnieper. That was to be our position over the winter, but to our surprise on the other side the Russians were already right in our face. We discovered that on the twentieth, many of their troops had already crossed the Dnieper.

It became clear to us that our winter encampment could not stay on the Dnieper, but instead closer to the Oder River in Silesia. We held our position from September twenty-seventh through October twelfth. On October twelfth, it was time for the dance to continue. We marched out from Dnipropetrovs'k, traveling between Krywyj Rih and Nikopol towards the city of Odessa. We marched about one hundred and thirty kilometers out from Dnipropetrovs'k and paused to assess the situation. Despite all of the obstacles we laid for our enemy, including blowing up bridges, mining road, and setting traps, they were always right on our heels. We stopped to make camp along a stretch of railroad near the railway station at Stjesabudinov. We stayed there for a few days to take a break from our enemy's pursuit, but we were out in the open along the railway. On the other side of the tracks lay a village by the name of Brandk. We scouted the town and determined that would be a better defensive position. There we could take shelter and not be so exposed to bad weather.

[I was never able to identify the two towns that Oskar called "Stjesabudinov" and "Brandk". I cannot say if they are the correct names of the locations.]

Chapter 6 BETRAYED BY MY GERMAN BOOTS

On October twentieth, we received the orders to prepare for an attack on Brandk. The town was lightly defended and the assault was quick and successful. Our new position was significantly better than being out in the open on the train tracks.

The next day I fell ill with Tonsillitis. I checked myself in with the doctor and I stayed for a few days with the support line. On the twenty-seventh, the battalion commander sent for me. He told me that things were falling apart, and when I was on my feet again he needed me back in service. As soon as I arrived back at the camp, I went to see the commander. He asked me about my health and I told him that everything was back to normal. The commander made it clear to me that the Russians were preparing for another attack. He ordered me to go to the watch post and listen carefully because I understood Russian.

I prepared for my assignment and left for the watch post at one thirty in the early morning, on October twenty-eighth. It was a very dark night. Thick clouds blocked any light from the moon or stars. It was difficult at first to get my bearings, but after walking around for a short time I became quite familiar with the area. I ventured further away from the village and out into the fields for about one and a half kilometers until I came within sight of the Russian line. They were camped at the edge of a corn field.

I crept through the rows of corn, and settled into a lookout point that offered a clear sight path where I could keep my eyes on the Russian troops. I was not alone. As I approached the spot, I saw a comrade of mine from the fifth company. He had also found the location advantageous and already positioned himself there. It was so dark that if I hadn't called out to him, he would not have seen me. I asked him twice where the sixth company's base camp was. He answered me only by glancing off to the right. I understood the direction, but by this time the fog was so dense that you could hardly see two meters in front of you. The weather conditions were strange. The fog was shifting, sinking down as deep as fifty centimeters from the ground and rising at times two meters above. The front was very still, like the calm before the storm.

With my prime lookout spot already occupied, I continued my patrol, heading in the direction of the base camp. At one point the fog lifted, revealing an image that made me freeze in my tracks. It was the sight of the silhouettes of two men standing just thirty meters in front of me. I determined right away that these were not our men and that I must be very close to our enemy. I signaled a warning for the military police to send guards to my location. I knew they heard me. I quickly dropped to the ground for cover, took out my S8, and fired upon them in a rampage. They fired back. A minute or two into the skirmish I noticed blood running down from my right hand. I had been hit, but it wasn't bad.

I stayed low to the ground for another few minutes under some brush, but I was in a very vulnerable spot. If I remained here I'd be dead before too long. I readied myself to make a dash out of the cover. To the left I heard the footsteps of our MPs behind me. The shooting caught their attention, and I was relieved to know that help was on the way. It was impossible for me to move out, because as soon as I raised my head I heard bullets whistle past my ears. For the time being, it was better to lay still and wait them out. The fog was beginning to lift again. I looked at my watch and it was now three o'clock.

About twenty meters away I could make out a faint puff of black smoke. It looked like I wasn't the only one in the area pinned down by the Russians. I decided that area offered me better protection where I could get myself oriented and determine exactly where I was. I jumped up out of my cover and ran as fast as I could. The Russians fired at me and I felt the wake of several shots wiz past me, but I kept on going. When I got close enough to the new shelter I dove head first inside. I was relieved to have made it without being hit, and for a moment I felt safe.

I rolled over, sat up and looked around. Six faces stared back at me. I also saw a grenade launcher. One of the men looked at me and spoke in a clear, Russian voice "Hey, are you alright?"

My heart sank deep into my chest. I knew that I was absolutely not alright. What had I done?

I was wearing a black fur coat that I had picked up many months ago and a big, Russian winter cap. The six soldiers inside believed that I was also a Russian soldier. I certainly looked that way in my outfit. I gave the man slight nod, but said nothing. I tried heard to conceal my anxiety. I had to get out of there and fast. I started to climb back out of the shelter. One of the men inside took note of the boots I was wearing and recognized them as part of a German military uniform. He grabbed me by the leg and pulled me back in, shouting "It's a god damn Fritz!" Soon I felt the grip of many hands dragging me to the ground. The men surrounded me, took my weapon and made me raise my hands. One of them pulled the fur coat off of me, turned me around, and went through all my pockets. They took my wallet and its contents, grabbed my watch, and then ripped out all of my awards: the E.K. Sturmabzeichen, a Romanian medal, and my silver badge for being wounded in action. The Russians studied them all carefully, beaming with pride over their catch. When they were satisfied with their trophies they dragged me from the hideout to present me to the company leader, who was only about one hundred meters away.

Upon our arrival at the Russian camp, three guards took over my watch. The men searched my pockets again, finding a lighter, a mirror, and a comb. The commander approached us and without a word took the comb for himself. Then he picked up my Soldbuch, a booklet given to every soldier with a detailed account of his assignments, weapons issued, and other valuable information. He leafed through it, but couldn't make anything of it. He looked in my direction and studied me top to bottom. He seemed puzzled by my appearance. I supposed it was because I did not carry a rank on my jacket and had no insignia on my shoulder.

"Are you an officer?" he asked.

"No, I am a cook, just an ordinary cook for the troops." I knew that I could tell him anything, because I saw that he did not understand what was written in my Soldbuch. He took two steps toward me and struck me in the face with the book. He handed it back to me and said "Take this you [expletive]".

The commander turned to the guards. "Bring this Fritz back to the rest of the battalion. And stay alert. I don't want him to escape."

In a chorus they all answered "Yes, commander." One of the guards pressed his weapon in my back. "Raise your hands over your head." I complied in a smooth and unthreatening motion. Another guard shoved me in the back to get me moving, staying behind me with the one who acquainted me with his rifle. The third guard walked about three meters in front of me, making it clear that I should follow him. The darkness of the early morning hour together with the dense fog made it difficult to keep him in view, even at that proximity.

I was fidgeting as I walked. I couldn't get my mind off of my Soldbuch. That would be a valuable record to my enemy once they are able to read it. I must get rid of it, but how? As we walked, the Russians trailing me were engaged in a lively conversation and started to fall further behind. Trying hard to be as inconspicuous as possible I reached for my Soldbuch and gently tugged it out of my left side pocket. When I pulled it out I tossed it onto the ground. Then I stomped on it, tearing it apart with my boots and smashing it in the mud. Though it was hard to see through the darkness and the fog, the Russians were surprised by the rustling and rushed toward me. One of them jumped on me, knocking me to the ground. He struck me repeatedly with a flask on the small of my back. When he was satisfied with his work he got up and shouted, "Stand up! Quickly! Or I will shoot you right here."

I groaned as I got to my feet. "What where you doing?" he asked, but I did not reply. He hit me again with the back of his rifle, but not hard enough to knock me over. "Now move! If you do that again you're a dead man, understand?" Again I said nothing. Though my back hurt I managed a smile. The excitement abruptly ended the conversation. Their footsteps were much closer now.

The darkness and fog both lifted as we marched through fields of corn and wheat. The sunlight greeted our arrival in a nearby village where the Russians had established a battalion combat post. One of the three men watching me reported in to the command station. The other two stayed outside with me. They looked conspicuously alert, as they knew they were now in the company of their superiors. The first guard soon came back out to get me, led me through the front door, and presented me to the commander. Inside the post a great number of officers and other crewmen gathered around me. At first I found all the attention quite amusing and I gave out a short laugh out loud. The gravity of my situation soon enveloped me and washed the smile from my face.

The battalion leader ordered a sergeant to search me. I was forced to undress down to my underwear. Once more they went through all of my pockets and all of the seams of my clothing. Two men carefully rubbed their hands through the lining of my felt boots. Of course they found nothing, as I had already been thoroughly ransacked twice before. When they were satisfied, they picked up my clothing and threw it back at me.

The battalion commander took a few steps closer to me, slowly enough to afford me some time to hastily put my clothes back on. When he reached me he asked in German "Where are your papers?"

I looked him in the eye and replied "The company leader had already taken them."

The commander looked back at the team leader and asked "Is this true?"

The nervous officer replied "Yes, commander. We did take them. I must have given them to someone, or maybe I put them down someplace. I will search for them."

"Yes, you will."

The team leader bowed his head slightly then dashed out of the room.

The commander again turned his attention to me. "Are you an officer?"

"No. I am an ordinary soldier and a cook. This is my first deployment."

He smiled back and me and walked a few steps behind his desk. Then he unrolled a piece of paper and laid it before me. It was a map of the entire region. It showed the Russian front line and the exact positions of all the divisions and where the companies were located.

"Are you familiar with this area?" he asked.

"No, I am not."

He looked over my shoulder at the other officers in the room and said in Russian "This [expletive] is playing dumb. I don't have time for this. Take him back to the division." The guard grabbed me by the arm as I finished the last of my buttons and escorted me to a small room at the post where they held me for another five hours. At two o'clock in the afternoon, a different guard retrieved me from my cell and led me out of the building. Two other soldiers were waiting for me outside.

The division was stationed twenty kilometers from the village, deeper into Russian territory. The three men accompanied me as we marched on foot. We arrived there at six o'clock in the evening. One of them ran ahead to notify the guard at the gate that we had arrived. Once inside the camp, we marched straight to the office of the division commander. He was a colonel. One of the soldiers passed the commander a note. He read it silently, looked up at me and smiled. I wondered if the smile was from seeing me or the note. The commander walked up to me, got right in my face, and in a threatening tone bellowed, "You will start answering questions."

That didn't shock me at all, but I also knew that things were going to get serious now. He walked around me as I stood still. He asked me over and over again, "Where are your papers?" Each time I replied that they were taken from me by someone in the company. The line appeared to be working for me, so I stuck with it.

This repeated for a few minutes before he turned away and shouted "I'm done with this. Just lock him up." Two of the guards flanked me and escorted me to the next house. As we walked inside, they presented me to a man who I learned was the lead prison warden of the division. He was sitting at a desk in a room at the front of the house. There were three women with him. I hadn't seen many women among the Russian troops. I'm sure he was proud to surround himself with them, but in reality they were each so ugly. They looked like hyenas. There was also a man, a Russian civilian, who I later learned was the owner of the house.

The warden got up from his desk and walked over to me. He had only one question, "Are you sending packages of stolen items back home?" That was a question I hadn't expected. I gave no answer. The civilian followed up and asked, "You Fritz, did you steal that fur coat?"

What kind of questions were these? I didn't answer him either. I couldn't help think that everyone here was so stupid.

Chapter 7   THE PRISON CELL

"Have it your way," groaned the warden. He unlocked a strong door that opened into a dark room and tossed me inside. He quickly secured the door behind me. I turned around to find myself in a cell with five other prisoners, all Russian. Three of them were in German uniforms and came from the Vlasov army. The other two were civilians. They were formerly Ukrainian policemen that were discovered to be abating the Germans. The men knew right away that I was a German soldier. They were staring up at me, but I looked away from them and walked to a corner on the other side. I stood quietly staring at the wall. The others were silent as well. How long could I refuse to cooperate before they lose patience? More importantly, what would happen to me when that time comes? I seemed to have a long time now to think on these questions.

The date was October thirtieth. By nightfall we were all very tired, and everyone lied down to sleep. We spent the night together in that cold cell, huddled close to preserve heat. I still had not said a word to any of them. At seven o'clock in the morning I heard the key at the lock. The door creaked loudly as it opened just enough to allow a beam of light to pierce the darkness, then it quickly slammed shut. An hour later the door opened again, this time more deliberately. The owner of the house had come to bring us breakfast, a bowl of soup with six spoons and six slices of bread. There was a woman with him. The warden came in as well and stood over us. "Eat up!" he barked. I was not in the mood to eat and I refused the meal. He said to me, "Ah that's too easy for you!" He looked at the woman and said, "This man needs to eat from his own plate. Bring him one." She left but quickly returned with a plate and a German spoon. I was the only one who was given a wooden spoon. I wasn't hungry, but I wanted to acknowledge his sensitivity to my German heritage. Still seated on the floor, I looked him in the eye and nodded in appreciation. I took the plate and ate up. He smiled and said, "Culture is culture." With that, he and the woman disappeared behind the door and locked us back in.

At twelve o'clock, the warden returned. The light of the sun shining in through the door into the dark cell blinded us for a moment. He held a note in his hand with two names written on it. He read the names and the two former policemen stood up. He handed each a spade and ordered them outside. When the door closed, the four of us looked at each other. We knew what the spade was for. They would be coming for us next. After an hour, the two men returned. The warden opened the doors and shoved them inside. They collapsed to the ground, beaten and bruised. The three other prisoners asked them what they had done. They answered with in a shaky voice that they were forced to dig holes, but that was all.

We knew what would happen next. One of us will be the first one to land in one of those holes. The Russians talked quietly amongst themselves, and I heard them saying that the 'Fritz' was probably next. Two hours later the warden was back with more names. Without pause he called out the three men from the Vlasov troops. In an instant their expression changed. They looked sorrowfully at each other, believing they only had a few moments more to live. They sat on the floor with tears in their eyes, staring up at six Russian soldiers who took no pity on them as they yanked them off their feet and dragged them outside. The warden left with them. The cell was silent now, each of us straining to hear the sounds coming from outside that might foretell our own fate. About five minutes later the silence was pierced by several gunshots, followed by a dreadful scream. I closed my eyes tightly, as if that would hide me from the scene outside. One of the assassins clearly did not hit his target cleanly. That would soon be remedied with another gunshot, this one from a pistol. Then all was quiet again. I opened my eyes and looked at my remaining two cell mates. They looked back at me apologetically, as if they believed their digging made them complicit in the execution. One of them spoke directly to me for the first time. "They were in the garden near the house, about a hundred meters out. That's where we dug the holes."

I wanted to say something to make them feel better, but all I could offer in return was "It's okay."

The silence outside that followed was disturbed only by the occasional sound of footsteps and hushed voices. I became very warm and started to sweat. Though it was cold in the cell, I took off my fur coat, tossed it to the ground, and loosen my clothing. I paced back and forth two or three times, but it offered me no comfort. I walked to the corner of the room and slumped to the ground. I stared down at the dirt floor and said to myself aloud in German, "It's so strange."

I picked my head up and saw the men looking back at me, clearly waiting for me to continue. I thought it polite to carry on in Russian. "So strange to think this is where my life would end. I had accepted that my death was a likely outcome when I joined the army. I am not afraid of death, but I had hoped for a more meaningful end to my life than this. My family will likely never learn of my whereabouts. In time, they will assume that I had been killed. My comrades from my battalion will only know that I disappeared one evening while on patrol. They will record my name as a soldier who was missing in action and never found. As my battalion moves on from this part of the front, I will be simply one less person who makes the trip. There will be no marker of my remains and likely no record of my capture to show that I had been here. I will have been simply erased. What an odd ending."

One of them said, "It's not over yet."

I let out a short chuckle. "Yes, you're right. It's not over yet."

I sat quietly in the corner waiting for my turn. I didn't have to wait long. The warden was back. He unlocked the door and opened it just wide enough to stretch his arm out into the room to point his finger at me. "You, come," he said.

I jumped to my feet and straightened myself up. The door swung open a bit wider and I saw that the division commander was with him. "Pick up your coat" ordered the commander.

I walked toward the door saying, "It's not much use to me anymore."

"Take it with you!" he barked. "It's cold and nasty outside. There is a storm with a mixture of snow and rain." I was not in the mood for an argument. I turned to pick my coat off the floor, draped it over my shoulders, and followed the commander. As we walked outside, I looked around for the guards with the riffles. I was surprised to find none. I followed him through the camp and into a house where a Lieutenant was waiting for me. I removed my coat and he offered me a chair. I sat at the front of his desk and looked at him, puzzled as to what he could want.

The officer pulled out a map and started drawing on it. I sat quietly observing the young lieutenant work earnestly on his creation. As I watched, I felt less tense as this didn't look like the makings of an execution. It seemed as though he was at it for almost an hour, and I enjoyed watching him work. He was actually quite good; I could see he knew a thing or two about art. He was also very friendly. He offered me a cigarette, which I gladly took, and asked if I had a chance to clean myself up today.

It became clear to me what was happening. It appeared that Russians wanted to use me as a messenger to deliver false troop information back to the Germans. My cellmate was correct, it isn't over yet. When he was finally finished he gestured to me that I should pick it up, and I did.

After I had taken the drawing, the person assigned to watch me escorted me into the next room to the division commander. Though he didn't walk close to me, the stench of alcohol from his breath was overwhelming and even walking this short distance he managed to stumble. This guy must be a horrible soldier. I hoped there were many more like him in this camp. Soon I was back in the presence of my good friend the colonel. Knowing that they planned to keep me alive for at least a little while longer, I was not intimidated.

"Sit here" he said, pointing to a chair at the head of his desk. I took my seat and watched as he laid before me yet another map that showed where the division was located.

"Be reasonable with me and answer some questions. We can do this the easy way or the hard way, but one way or another we are going to force you to speak."

"Alright," was all I said.

"Now, how large was the company that you came from?"

I answered quickly "Ninety-five men strong."

He thumped his fist on the map and yelled "Don't lie to me! I know for a fact your company had only twenty-five men."

I calmly replied, "If you already knew exactly then why are you asking me?" Before I was captured, my company did indeed have ninety-five men. In reality, the company now had only twelve.

He got up off his chair and paced around me angrily, clearly trying to contain his temper.

"Where are your papers? Are you an officer?"

I answered again, "I am only a cook, just an ordinary soldier."

He laughed at me scornfully. "Goddamn Germans. In the whole German army I can find no snipers, no battalion leaders, and no officers, only cooks."

He walked to the door, opened it, and shouted so loudly that you could hear it from a kilometer away, "Get out of here!"

I calmly got up and without looking at him walked to the door. As I passed him he said, "Have it your way, Fritz. Tomorrow we'll get you to talk and I promise you it will be a whole lot less pleasant."

Private vodka-breath was waiting for me outside to deliver me back to the warden. As we walked the guard struck me twice in the back with a club, muttering something I could not understand. I let it go. He handed me off to the warden then led me back into the cell. I was relieved to find that my two Russian cell mates were still alive and waiting for me. Before he closed the door, he leaned in close to me and offered a piece of advice.

"I don't know who you are, but as you lay here tonight you should think carefully about following orders shouted at you from the colonel." With that the warden took his leave, and the door slammed behind me.

The two prisoners quickly got up off the ground. Their faces beamed with an incredulous look.

"Are you hurt?" asked one of the men. He was tall and muscular with blonde hair, and spoke quietly in Russian. I simply replied, "No."

"What did they do to you?" he continued.

I didn't answer right away. The prisoner glanced at his other cell mate then moved a bit closer to me. "My name is Rischa. He is Ivan." I looked at Ivan and he gave me a slight nod. Ivan was a bit shorter than Rischa with black hair and a thin face. "Where did they take you?"

I decided it was safe for me to answer their questions. "They took me to see the division commander. They tried to get information out of me about our troop position."

"How many guards did you see?" Rischa asked.

"Not many. It appears to be a small post. But I didn't see much. The one assigned to watch me was quite drunk."

Rischa and I continued to talk for a while and I began to sense that the two were plotting something. After a short time, Rischa stood up and walked back to Ivan, who remained in the far corner of the cell. They turned to converse quietly amongst themselves. I heard Rischa tell Ivan to ask me if I would join in. Ivan looked up at me and gestured for me to come closer to him. I crawled along the floor to the other side of the room next to the two men.

"We're getting out of here," said Ivan. "Tonight. You're welcome to join us."

I looked at him quizzically and asked "How is that possible? There is a guard right outside the door and a few others not far away."

Ivan answered "Don't concern yourself with that. I'm telling you we're getting out of here anyway".

I didn't take long to think it over for myself. "Okay. Let me know how I can help."

"For now just stay close and remain quiet."

Rischa went to work on our escape. He had found a horseshoe in the garden while he and Ivan were digging what would become the graves of the Vlasov soldiers. He kept it hidden under his coat. Rischa lay down on the cell floor along the outside wall that faced the garden and began to quietly scrape the horseshoe along the wall. It was easy work as the walls were made of clay. Ivan laid down on his left side and listen for movement in the room next door. I was on Rischa's right side, along a wall that was against a barn where they kept horses. Ivan and I listened carefully for any noises outside. We could hear that the guards were changed regularly. A new guard would replace the old one and would open the door to the cell to make sure we were all still inside. We kept track of changes in the guard and cleverly determined that it was about ten o'clock. Shortly after the last guard change occurred and having checked on us, Rischa had already managed to make a big hole in the wall. We felt the cold air rush into the cell and knew our plan was working. A few minutes later, the scraping had stopped. Rischa turned to face us. He was covered in dust, but that couldn't hide the enthusiasm on his face. "It's time to get out of here,." he said.

Lying on his back, Rischa squeezed himself through the opening in the wall that he created, pulling with him chunks of clay as he slid himself along. In a moment he was gone, taking his first step to freedom. We heard his voice through the gap as he called out to Ivan, "Run!" but it was me who crawled out next. Ivan followed close behind. When I emerged outside in the wet snow and mud, I got to my feet quickly to make way for Ivan. The weather was very bad, but it was gripped by the excitement of freeing myself from our captors. It was very dark with a hint of a moon behind the clouds. We tiptoed silently through the village streets, ducking around houses and barns until we got to the edge of town, careful not to be seen. There were a series of trenches along parts of the perimeter of the town. They appeared to be empty, and with good reason. We were twenty or more kilometers deep into Russian-held territory, and the houses in town were much more comfortable and inviting for the troops than staying in a cold, muddy trench. We scampered down and walked carefully through the trenches until we reached the end, where we climbed back out and quietly slipped away into the open fields.

The sky was very dark and there was hardly any light, but my new Russian friends were very familiar with the area. That was fortunate for me because I could hardly tell which direction I was headed in. We didn't speak a word to each other as we hiked twelve kilometers through fields of withering corn stalks and trampled crops until we arrived at a small village. *[I was never able to identify the name. Oskar called it Hevreskipossolek].* This was their goal. With the village in sight, we paused to look carefully around the area before proceeding. Rischa approached me and put his hand on my shoulder.

"My sister lives here. She will be able to help us and get us something to eat."

I nodded in agreement. "That's good." I was beginning to wonder what our next move was going to be. It won't be long before the Russian army discovers we are missing. In fact, I'm sure they already know.

Ivan noticed our conversation and walked back to join us. "They'll be looking for us very soon," he said. "We will not be able to outrun them. Rischa, I saw a patrolman. They're here, in town. We must stay out of their sight."

Rischa gestured to Ivan that we continue on. I gently grabbed Rischa by the arm and gave his sleeve a tug. I looked him in the eye and offered a faint smile to acknowledge my gratitude for his assistance.

When we approached the village, we stayed off the streets so as not to run into any patrols. It was about one o'clock in the morning when we arrived at the house where his sister lived. Her name was Maruscha. We walked to the back of the house and Rischa rapped gently on the back door. We waited a while until Maruscha arrived. She peered carefully out the window, recognized her brother and opened the door for us. The three of us dove inside, closed the door, and turned off the light.

"Rischa what was going on?" she asked. "Someone told me that the Russians had taken you to a prison." Rischa put his arm around her shoulder and walked her to the other side of the room where they spoke in hushed voices. Ivan and I stayed on the other side. I watched him pace back and forth across the dark room, waiting for the conversation to end. When they were done speaking, Maruscha turned to Ivan. Without a word she walked up to him, threw her arms around him, and greeted him with a warm hug and a kiss. That's when I learned that Maruscha also happened to be Ivan's girlfriend. She was living with a woman whose husband was in the war.

"I'll tell Mrs. Surra that you are here. They will be looking for you. Keep the lights off and don't make any noises. I'll take you up to the hayloft and you can stay there for the night. Then I'll get you something to eat."

Maruscha left the small room at the back of the house for a moment to inform the woman of our arrival. We waited silently in the darkness and the cold for Maruscha's return, blowing on our hands to get warm. When she came back, she took Ivan by the hand and brought us back outside to another entrance. The door opened to reveal only a narrow staircase that groaned with each step we took. The stairs led to a hayloft above the living quarters of the house. It was even colder up there but we were certainly out of sight.

"I'll be right back with something to eat." Maruscha turned to descend the creaky stairs. Rischa paused a moment, then followed after her. Ivan and I each laid claim to a corner of the loft and shaped the hay into a place to sit while we waited. I was looking forward to getting something to eat.

A few minutes later, we heard the door open and the sound of the stairs announcing Rischa's return. He gave us each a chunk of dried ham and some bread. He also brought a bottle of water, which we all drank from.

"Thank you, again," I said to him as I began to gnaw at the tough piece of meat.

"I spoke with Mrs. Surra," Rischa explained as he turned a piece of bread in his hands. "She is happy to help us. We can stay here for as long as we need."

Ivan responded. "She is a kind woman. I always liked her. But Rischa, you know that we can't stay up here for too long. They will find this house and surely they will look for us up here. This will be the first place they look."

"I know." Rischa took another bite of the bread. "But we do have some time. We can stay here for the night."

"Yes, we can" answered Ivan. "But not for much longer."

"Ivan, where are we going to go?" Rischa asked, not out of frustration but instead of concern for his safety and that of his friend. "Do you just want to wander around the country trying to stay one step ahead of the Russians? And what are we going to do for food? And what of Maruscha?"

"Relax, Tovarish. I know … I know. We just need to think this through."

I sat quietly while my new friends tried to figure out our next move. I was fortunate to have found them. They were familiar with the area and the dangers. I knew they would be a big help to me while I figured out my next move. I needed to get back to the German army, but I was now deep behind the enemy lines with no way of contacting my comrades. I stayed out of the conversation, but listened attentively. Rischa explained that when he spoke with Mrs. Surra, she told him that the Russian troops had moved in to town and now occupied a large area.

The two former police officers weighed their options. Being out in the open was too dangerous. We were in the middle of a large concentration of Russian troops who were looking for us. They went through names of people they knew. Aside from Maruscha and Mrs. Surra, the men concluded they could not trust anyone else in town. If we stayed in the house, we would surely be caught. This is the first place they would come look for us.

I could make out Rischa's silhouette against the dim light coming through the window. He grabbed the bottle of water and drank sparingly from it. Then he shared an idea. "We need to hide. Right here in the garden, outside the house. We'll build separate bunkers, for each of us. Mrs. Surra and Maruscha will take care of us. They can keep us fed. We'll hide here until the danger has subsided."

"It would buy us some time" answered Ivan.

"We could be here for quite a while. But eventually the army will move out. They have to. The front line is always shifting."

"Yes" said Ivan. "That seems to be our best option. Oskar, what do you think?"

I nodded in agreement.

"Good" said Ivan. "We'll stay here in the hayloft tomorrow. Then at night we will begin building our bunkers. We'll have to work at night."

The two fell quiet again. Eventually, we all flattened out a spot in the hay to lie down and sleep. It was cold but I was comfortable in my long, black fur coat.

Chapter 8   STAYING OUT OF SIGHT

We woke up when the morning light came through the dusty window and narrow gaps of the wall boards of the hayloft, but it was not our time to get up. Maruscha brought us some breakfast, but Ivan told her not to come back to the hayloft again until dark, so as not to arouse suspicion. We waited patiently for the night to come. We spoke very little, but were comfortable in each other's silence. For a while, I was angry with myself for making the mistake of diving into that Russian hideout without knowing where I was going, and allowing myself to be captured. Eventually I assured myself that when you're in a fight, you need to make quick life-and-death decisions and rarely have the luxury of sufficient time to think through every action and possible outcome. I became comfortable in the realization that I did what I felt at the time gave me the best chance of survival, and gained a tactical advantage in the skirmish. In the end, I was lucky to have found these two men so willing to help me, sharing their food and shelter.

As the day passed, I pondered my next steps. It came down to two things: avoid being re-captured by the Russians, and survive long enough to find an opportunity to rejoin the German army. For the time being I placed, my fate in the hands of two fugitives I barely knew.

Night came and Rischa announced it was dark enough to begin our work. We climbed out into the yard and walked around the house to survey the area. We were looking for an inconspicuous spot to build the hide out, and the materials we would need for the job. I let the two former policemen lead the effort. After a few minutes, they settled on a spot and each of us began building our bunker. They were constructed with logs we found from around the yard and straw from the horse's barn. There was a small shack just two meters from the barn that held a cow. It was built in the same fashion as the barn, and we incorporated that structure in our plan as well. Rischa built his bunker at the end of the horse's stall, Ivan built his in front of the shack, and mine was in between them. The entrance to our bunkers was through a round tunnel in the horse's stall under the feed trough.

We worked through the night. When we were done, we paced around our hidden compound several times, looking at it from different angles. After a few circles around the small barn, Rischa and Ivan looked at each other and smiled, then turned to me and did the same. We were proud of our work. I have to say the bunkers were very well built and it was clear my new Russian friends were masters at this. We were so well hidden that from the yard above, you could not recognize anything. Daylight would soon be upon us, time to put our efforts to the test. We each climbed in and crawled to our spot that would become our new home. For how long, we did not know.

I settled in and paused for a moment to take stock of my new shelter. It was cramped, as there was very little room to stretch my arms and legs. The air was stuffy and damp, but the hay we brought inside helped to make us more comfortable. More than anything it was dark. There was not even the faintest hint of light. The total absence of light was difficult to get used to at first, but in time I learned to be comfortable with it.

Earlier that evening Maruscha left the house to inform Rischa's wife of our situation. His wife lived in on the other side of town, about two kilometers away. About an hour after we had settled in to our shelters, probably around three o'clock in the morning, we enjoyed a meal in our bunkers for the first time with the food that Mrs. Surra brought to us. After that I tried to get some sleep, but that proved to be quite difficult. I kept having the sensation that something was crawling over me. Being holed up like a rodent underground, it's a good bet that things were indeed crawling all over me while I lay there on my bed of hay. The air was also damp and stale. We made sure that each bunker was vented to let some fresh air into the space, but the atmosphere also took some time to get used to.

Eventually I did get to sleep. When I awoke I could see that it was far along in the day, as the sun seemed to be quite high in the sky. The near total absence of light in our bunker made the transition of night and day, and back to night almost meaningless. The day passed again into night. The three of us could communicate between our bunkers, but we hardly spoke a word. We had no way of knowing if anyone was outside and able to hear us, so we agreed that we would be safest if we kept silent during the day.

The first days we spent in our bunkers were the worst. During the daytime it became very warm in our hideout, so much so that there were times when I removed all of my clothing. I was also covered with lice and I could not stop scratching. As a result my body was coated with blisters from the heat and the scratching. On the third day I asked Mrs. Surra for an oil lamp so I can be rid of these lice and treat my blisters. I couldn't take it anymore. She brought me the lamp, but I gave up on the idea quickly as there were no matches to be found to light the lamp.

The three women assumed the duty of keeping us fed and safe. Maruscha took care of her boyfriend, Ivan, Rischa's wife took care of her husband, and I was cared for by Mrs. Surra. There was enough room in the bunker for each of our caregivers to crawl in, bring us our food, and keep us company for a while.

Meals were served to us in the mornings at five o'clock and in the evenings at ten o'clock under cover of darkness. In the morning we had one kilogram of bread, soup, a glass of water, Brussels sprouts, and from time to time a meatball or some turkey. In the evening if we were lucky, we had roasted potatoes with a fried egg and water. On occasion we were treated to Samogon, which is Russian moonshine.

Mrs. Surra would crawl inside with my meal and sit in the darkness with me while I ate. She was quite eager for my attention and I was happy to give it to her. When I was finished she would stay and we would talk, a little bit longer each day. With so little room for the two of us, there was no other option than to sit practically on top of each other. On the third day, she stayed with me for a very long time. I put my arm around her and she rested her head on my shoulder as we chatted.

I never did get a good look at her face in the daylight. She seemed fairly attractive, but I suppose in the darkness after not having spent time with any woman in over two years that every female would seem attractive. (The exception was those three women back at the Russian command post. It would take many more years of captivity

to get to the point when anyone would find them attractive.)
Mrs. Surra was probably in her early thirties, the same age as
I was. I had the feeling that she was at one time heavier, but
when food became harder to come by as the war raged
through the country, she had probably lost a bit of weight.
She shared stories of her husband with me. He had been
gone for over two years and it had been more than a year
since she had last heard from or about him. She resigned
herself to the fact that he was probably never coming back.
She told me about his drinking and how he would come
home intoxicated after a night at the tavern and abuse her. I
listened carefully without interruption while she did all the
talking.

Both of her arms were tightly wrapped around me by
the time she had finished. I kissed her forehead as we
snuggled quietly together for a few more minutes.

"I am very grateful to you" I said. You're risking
your life for me. You understand that if I am caught we will
both be shot."

She put her hand on my cheek. "I will keep you safe
until this is all over, until the end of the war. You can stay
right here."

Six days had past and I had not seen a ray of
sunshine. I asked Mrs. Surra how much longer I need to sit
here, but she kept telling me to hold on and that everything
will turn out alright. I wanted to get at least an hour of fresh
air each day, but my caregiver kept me from doing that and
insisted I stay hidden. During her visits with me at meal
time, she would bring me news of the war that she head from
Russian soldiers. Many more Russian troops had moved in
to completely occupy the town and surrounding area. She

told me that German captives were often seen being led through the streets. The news got me so agitated. I wanted to get back out there and fight alongside my comrades. It bothered her to hear me say those things, so over time she stopped bringing me any more news.

Days passed into weeks. All I could do was sit in my shelter, keep safe, and trust in the people that were caring for me. As the time dragged on, I grew impatient. There seemed to be no end to the Russian occupation of this place. While my two comrades seemed perfectly content to ride out the time in the bunkers, I was not. Regardless of the conditions outside they were home. I was far from it. They were with their loved ones. I needed to rejoin my battalion.

In the afternoon of December fifteenth, there was a commotion outside, and the monotony of the days spent in hiding was shattered. I heard a loud conversation coming from the yard. I could not make out exactly what was being said, but there was a man who was clearly angry about something. Then I heard him shout in a demanding voice "Where are they?" Maruscha replied curtly "There's no one here!" I heard footsteps come closer and the clang of a shovel as the man began to dig near the horses' stall. Then there was the sound of a second shovel scraping the dirt, as another man had joined the effort. The whole area was being turned over. We sat motionless, hoping we would remain undetected. I could not see anyone, but I knew they close, really close. After a while, the digging stopped. The men found nothing because the bunkers were located above the stalls, not under the ground. It fell quiet again, but here in our bunkers we were all on edge. Time stood still. Every minute was like an hour. We seemed to dodge a bullet today. It took several more long and anxious hours before we were informed of what had transpired.

Well after darkness fell, at last we heard Maruscha's voice. She brought us something to eat and told us later that night she will bring more. She said that the neighbor had given us away, informing the authorities that someone must be hiding in the stalls, because people were always bringing food out there. Maruscha suggested that we leave the area in two days. She had relatives in a town about thirty kilometers from here who could keep us safe. The NKVD was now after us and she feared they would return. That night I was so nervous that I could not sleep. I was finally going to leave this place, but it would not be on my terms.

The next morning before the sun came out Maruscha brought us all a bit to eat. It wasn't much, but she said that this evening there would be more. Ten hours passed before I heard Maruscha and Rischa's wife come by to take care of their men. Maruscha leaned close to my bunker and told me quietly that Mrs. Surra will come for me in an hour. But just ten minutes later I heard the sound of a gunshot and the angry voices of several men. The NKVD was back and they were now very close to the stalls. I heard one man's voice yell "Come out!" I froze still. For a moment nobody moved. Then someone fired a few shots from a pistol into the ground before us and screamed "Get out of there right now!"

I heard Rischa and Ivan slowly climb out of their bunkers. They were discovered and overpowered, and had no choice but to surrender. I was petrified, wondering if they would also order me out of my hiding place. I waited to see what would happen, but there was no order directed at me. Now I could only wait … would Ivan and Rischa betray me?

A few more moments passed in silence. It seemed as though no one was paying attention to me. Though I heard no more voices, there was the sound of the shuffling of feet outside and then footsteps leading away from the house. The yard became very quiet. An hour had passed without further incident. I was beginning to believe that I had survived, when suddenly I heard footsteps coming towards the entrance to my hideout. I was convinced that I indeed had been betrayed. I braced for the worst but was relieved to hear Mrs. Surra's voice. "Oskar, it's me" she whispered. She crawled inside and put her arms around me. She was nervous and still sobbing, panting as she told me what had happened.

"It *was* the neighbor. He was convinced that we were hiding fugitives. He sought out an NKVD officer and told him that they would find someone here in the yard. Why would he do such a thing? We always got along so well."

"It's the war," I said softly. "It puts so much pressure on everyone's lives. The stress comes out in different ways. Perhaps he wanted to distance himself from any involvement in case someone was caught."

She was still crying. I held her tightly. "It's okay, we're safe for now. We need to stay quiet outside."

I said nothing more for a while until she calmed down.

"Oskar, when the NKVD arrived yesterday to search the yard they came out empty-handed. But they didn't leave. Instead, they stayed in the area to keep watch over the yard. When the two later came to bring out something to eat, that's when the agents ran in. I saw the whole thing from the window. They ran up to the yard, seized the girls, and ordered the men to come out of their hiding places. They didn't know about you. Once the two had crawled out, the officers carried all four of them away."

"That was very merciful of them not to give me away."

She paused for a moment before whispering "Oskar, they're all dead."

"They're dead?"

"Dead. Executed. Right in the center of town. Right away."

She leaned into me and I held her in my arms.

"I'm so sorry." With my free hand I reached out and grabbed a branch that we had incorporated into the wall of the bunker. I clenched it tightly.

"They did so much for me, and I barely knew them. I owe them so much. Those Russian bastards!" I snapped the branch and it startled her.

"I must get out of here. Tonight. You're in danger. They'll come back for you. You know this. I need to get far away from you."

"Yes, I know" she answered, "but not tonight. Don't leave tonight. It's too dangerous. Wait until tomorrow."

"You're right. Tomorrow it is. But now you must go. You don't know who may have seen you. Go back in the house. Please."

She gave me a kiss and slowly backed out of the bunker through the tunnel. She left me my dinner wrapped in a small hand towel on the floor of the bunker. For a while I just sat still, too upset to eat. Eventually I unwrapped the food that she left for me and ate. It was the first meal in many weeks that I did not share with my comrades. I curled up in a ball in the hay and went to sleep.

Daylight came and went. Once more I passed the time in my bunker sitting still, hoping that the NKVD agents would not return to look for additional fugitives. When darkness came the following evening, I slowly crept out of my hideout. When I emerged in the open I began to feel very ill and disoriented. For the past seven weeks I had not breathed the fresh air or seen any direct light. Mrs. Surra saw me out of her kitchen window as I tumbled to the ground. I sat still on the soft earth for a few minutes taking slow, deep breaths to acclimate to the environment. When she came out of the house, she ran up to me asking "Are you alright?"

"Yes, I'm fine. I just need a moment."

"Stay right there" she ordered, and ran back into the house. She returned a short time later with a collection of items for me wrapped in a larger towel. She had prepared some food to take with me for my journey. I was very grateful for her gift. I looked up at her, smiled, and said "Thank you. Thank you very much for all you've done."

"Where will you go?" she asked.

"I was thinking about that. I decided that it is best for me to go in the direction of Dnipropetrovs'k. I believe it offers the best chance to meet up with the German army. The Wehrmacht had established a post in the city and it's likely that it's still in German hands."

As I began to get off the ground, she helped me to my feet. I took a few deep breaths and smiled at her. "See, good as new."

She turned me around and pointed in a direction that took me straight through the center of town. "The city is about one hundred and fifty kilometers away in that direction. Just keep walking that way. I have no doubt you will find it."

"Yeah, no doubt." I buttoned my coat and placed the bundle she made for me into one of my pockets. I turned to her and hugged her tightly. "Thank you for all you've done."

"Good luck, Oskar" she whispered in my ear. "Stay hidden and safe."

"When the war is over I promise I will find you. We will see each other again."

She took a half step back and smiled. "We shall see."

I began my walk through the village, being especially careful to stay out of the neighbor's sight. I made my way to the edge of town as quickly as I could, until I was out in the fields far away from any houses. Then I proceeded to search for the train tracks by circling the village until I came upon them. I was certain that the tracks would lead me straight through to Dnipropetrovs'k.

I walked all through the night following the railway line. The sky was very dark, and I only had the tracks as my guide. It felt good to move my legs again, but I soon grew weary of the walk as I had not used those muscles in many weeks. I could tell that I lost some strength from the ordeal. Still I resisted the urge to stop and rest as I needed to get to Dnipropetrovs'k as quickly as possible and minimize my time I spent out in the open behind enemy lines. Now and then I heard the sounds of an animal nearby, rustling in the dried leaves of the crop that had been sown several weeks before. The air was cold and that helped to keep me alert.

I estimated that I covered about fifty kilometers that evening. During my travel I came upon the place where the Russian front line had been. Though it was dark, I saw very clearly the same shelter where months ago I was captured because of my boots. That's where this whole ordeal began. I continued to wander through large fields of corn and Brussels sprouts. The early morning sun was beginning to rise. I was tired, but I pressed on.

I encountered still more reminders of the war along my path. I walked past the foxhole again where our combat sector had been. Then I passed close by the village at the front line where the Russians attacked us with their tanks. I stood there for a moment surveying the area. That was a bloody battle. We had suffered heavy casualties there. I saw the remains of the tanks we fired upon for the second time. As I looked around and walked through the area, I saw a great number of fallen soldiers, both Russian and German. I was surprised that the bodies had not yet been collected. Some of them showed signs that animals had begun to feed on the flesh. I needed to keep going.

Everywhere I went it was clear to me that our soldiers had been there. I saw signs, such as a steel German army helmet, and wanted to believe it was left there in order to guide me back. I needed to keep my distance from the railway tracks in the daylight and travel unnoticed through the fields. As the day progressed, the weather had turned very bad. It began to rain, gently at first, but then it grew into a steady downpour. The ground was now very soft and it was becoming very difficult to walk, especially on my tired legs. It felt like the whole field was stuck to the bottom of my boots. I had to be careful not to lose them in the mud with each step I took.

I was growing very thirsty, but there was no water to be found. I passed by an old artillery firing position and found some empty cartridges. Some of them were turned upright and had collected water so I drank from them.

A few kilometers later I came upon a village that was pretty badly shot up. The rain had stopped, but I was still very wet. I decided to approach the village as it seemed quite deserted. I thought that I may find something to eat and to drink there, and perhaps also find some shelter to rest. I walked up to a house that was partially destroyed. The top floor had been blown off. To my surprise I found a woman living inside. I approached her and noticed very soon that she seemed to be quite upset, probably due to the destruction of her house. I begged for a glass of water. She looked at me scornfully and would not give me any. She probably sensed I was a German even though I spoke Russian to her. I then imagined what the woman must have thought of me and I quickly moved away from the house. The woman turned and walked straight into the village; probably to tell the neighbors that there a German was nearby. I left there in a hurry. As I made my way out, I kept looking behind me to make sure I wasn't being followed. I never saw anyone, probably because there were no men around. All the men were all on the front line.

I learned not to go near the locals as they were very suspicious of strangers. I hiked back into the fields, far away from the roads and villages I passed by. As I traveled that day, I encountered many small cemeteries erected for my German comrades. I could also see that the Russians had disturbed some of the graves. Night fell upon me. I paused for a moment, standing underneath the wide open skies. It was a peaceful moment, even though the weather was dreadful. It had turned colder and snow was now falling. I reflected upon my plight and the series of events that led me to this place. How odd it seemed to me that I shall find myself here, alone, cold, hungry, and exhausted. I'm hundreds of miles from home, an enemy in a strange land. At any moment I could be captured or killed. I wished I were comfortably back in my house with my family.

I shook my head to come back into the moment and concentrate on the task at hand. I needed to find a safe place to hide myself to that I can get a bit of rest. I passed through a corn field where I came across an old trench. Feeling around in the dark I found a dry area and laid down on it. I was in a terrible snowstorm, but the trench was so deep that the wind blew right over it. I was so exhausted that I quickly fell asleep, despite being uncomfortably cold and wet.

I don't know how long I was out, but I was jarred from my sleep when a locomotive roared past. I opened my eyes and saw that it was daylight. I remained on the ground for a moment while I completed my transition from a deep sleep to the consciousness of the day. I fumbled through the package that Mrs. Surra had given me to pull out a bit of dried meat and bread. Both were hard and tough, but my empty stomach welcomed them.

My adventure continued as I got to my feet and began to climb out of the trench. I stopped near the surface and peaked carefully around in all directions to make sure I was alone. There was no one in sight. I crawled out onto the ground, stood up, and marched on. I had a vague notion of where I was headed because I saw the Luftwaffe pass overhead. It appeared to me that they were flying out from

Dnipropetrovs'k toward the Front. I did not know how far I had traveled or how much further I had to go, but I was fairly confident that I was heading in the right direction and would ultimately reach the safety of a German post.

A few hours later I came upon a group of men who were some distance away from me, but walking in my direction. I turned right to make my way toward a line of trees planted as a wind barrier between the fields in an attempt to avoid being seen by them. I reached the tree line and paused behind a large trunk, standing motionless while I observed them. They passed me by and I went unnoticed. When they were far enough away, I continued my walk.

The going got better as weather turned colder and the ground froze. The sun was shining and provided a bit of warmth. I walked the entire day without coming across any village in my path. The only signs of civilization I encountered were an occasional barn or small house that stood isolated in the fields, like a lonely island in an ocean of barren land. Evening came again and it was time to look for a place to stay for the night. For this night I picked out better accommodations, a hay stack. The hay was rolled up and left out in the open field. I slowly crawled inside, careful not to sink too deeply in it. I made a small hollow and after I climbed in covered up the entrance to hide myself. It was a comfortable night as it was fairly warm inside.

The following morning after a restful sleep, I got ready to trek the remaining kilometers back to Dnipropetrovs'k. My rations had nearly run out. I found a few kernels of corn on the ground to still my hunger. Finally in the distance, I saw the city of Dnipropetrovs'k. The site of the city rising out of the flat land provided a boost to my stride. I arrived at the edge of the city around four o'clock in the afternoon. The buildings became more numerous and clustered together as I walked further into the city center. I crept through the alleys, not knowing the state of things. I saw very few people in the streets. It was quiet. No one spoke. Only the sound of an occasional vehicle traveling past me broke the stillness. There were no signs of occupation from either the Germans or the Russians. The lack of any clue as to what was going on in the city was creepy. It felt dangerous. If I was wrong about coming here, I could find myself right back in a prison cell.

I came upon an area of the town that was familiar to me. I had been in Dnipropetrovs'k three times before. The most recent time was just a couple of months ago. Our division made camp in that city on the Dnieper for about two weeks after our retreat from Sloviansk. I got to know a few parts of the city and could make my way around. I looked for the street named "Polowei N-6" and quickly found it. There was a dentist on that street that I had once visited. Three months ago he laid a crown for me. We got to be friendly and I felt I could trust him. It was around five o'clock in the evening. I walked up the short set of stairs to the front door of the house and casually knocked. The dentist's daughter arrived to open it. She took one look at me then turned to call out to her mother "Mommy, there's a beggar at the door. Can I bring him a piece of bread?"

Her mother answered from the next room "Give him a few Rubles." The girl looked back at me and I smiled at her. "That's very kind of you, but I do not need any money."

Upon hearing my voice her mother immediately came to the door. She gently brushed her daughter aside, took me by the arm and yanked me into the house. She glanced around outside and down the streets before she closed the door behind us.

"Please, sit down" she said.

I sat in a nearby chair and looked around. The girl stood motionless in front of me, staring at me. The woman fidgeted for a moment then told her daughter "Go get your father." As the girl left to perform her task, the woman gave me an uncomfortable smile, looked away, and then sank into a chair as she stared down at the floor. Her husband, Nikolai, was in the room next door at work on a set of teeth. The daughter knocked on the door and quickly opened it. She went inside to give him the news. Nikolai came out right away. He walked right up to me and I stood up to greet him. He put his hands on my shoulders. "Oskar, so good to see you again!"

"Hello, Nikolai."

He took a half-step back to get a good look at me. "Oskar," he said "what has happened to you?"

"I will tell you everything, but first may I ask you for a glass of water?"

He turned away and walked to his liquor cabinet. "No water for you, Oskar." He poured me a glass of vodka instead. I gratefully accepted it, raised my glass to him, and drank up. His wife felt more at ease as she observed our interaction. She stood up from the chair, looked at me and said "You must be hungry."

"Yes." I answered. "Thank you again."

"I'll make us something to eat." She turned and went into the kitchen. Her daughter followed close behind.

Nikolai led me into the living room and told me to wait for him while he finished his work on the man who was surely wondering if Nikolai had forgotten about his teeth. I was happy to have a comfortable and peaceful moment in front of the fireplace in a house where I was, for the time being, sheltered from the authorities and nosey neighbors. Nikolai returned ten minutes later and sat next to me, eagerly waiting for me to tell him about my situation. I explained to him what had happened to me, about my capture, imprisonment, and escape. I trusted him; I had to if I were to find my way back to my division. In turn, Nikolai shared with me what was happening on the front. The German army had not returned to Dnipropetrovs'k as I expected. Instead, the Russians moved in and were now in control of the city. By this time the front line had moved east and was somewhere between Nikopol and Kryvyi Rih. I traveled all this way only to learn that I could find no safety here, either.

We talked some more about our experiences over the past few months. Soon Nikolai's wife called us into the kitchen for dinner. It was the most wonderful meal I had had since I left home in June. The warmth of the potatoes and vegetables felt so good in my belly. I made sure to gobble up every last crumb. By the time I was done, the plate was as clean as it was sitting in the cupboard. I could tell that the family was amused by this. When we finished, his wife brought us each a warm cup of coffee as we continued to sit together at the kitchen table and talk. After a few sips Nikolai motioned for his daughter to leave the table while the three of us discussed my plight.

I needed to leave the city, desperate to find my way back across the front line into German-controlled territory. Of course that would have me walking straight into the line of Russian forces and through the battle zone. It was a path that would surely lead to disaster for me. There was no way

I could safely navigate that. I couldn't stay here, either. Nikolai did not offer that to me and he was right not to do so. And even if he did I would not accept his offer. I had seen what happens to kind people who shelter me from the authorities. I would certainly not put his family in that kind of danger.

We talked about my options, but none of them were good. I was now deep into Russian territory. Traveling the great distances that now divided me from my troops on foot was foolish. The winter had come, and being out in the open was not only dangerous for the cold temperatures, but also it increased the chances that I would be caught. Traveling by bus or train was clearly not an option, especially for one without papers. As we started running out of suggestions, the conversation became thinner and more somber. I would be leaving here soon and back on the city streets. I had to come up with something.

Then Nikolai concocted a plan. He recognized it was a bit of a stretch but he thought it could work. He told me that since I can still speak Polish, I could enroll in the Polish army. There was an army post in town where I could ask to enlist. Once in the Polish army, I would stay out of Russian hands. His wife initially laughed at the idea, but as we talked through it she noted that once I was enlisted in the Polish army, it would be safe for me to be on the streets as I would have papers. That way I could travel across the area and eventually make my way to the German border.

I stroked my chin and gave both of them a glance. They were both looking back at me, waiting for my reaction. I put my head down again and stared at my coffee cup. It was crazy, but it seemed to provide me with my best opportunity for staying out of Russian hands. Without looking up I answered "I think that's a wonderful idea."

I knew that Nikolai and his wife were fond of me. I was struck again by the kindness of the people from this area that I have come to know, and the effort and sacrifices they made in order to care for me. It was uncomfortable for me to think on it, knowing that I had caused so much destruction in their land. I recalled our march back from Sloviansk when we destroyed and burned everything in our path. We caused so much harm to the ordinary people who lived there, people like Nikolai and his wife.

It was crazy to think that I would find the safety from the Russian army that I sought by walking straight into an army post of the Russian army. That itself would require a plan. I asked Nikolai if he could be so kind as to procure some Russian credentials for me. "I'll take care of it at once" he replied, and with that he got up from the table, put on his coat, and left the house.

His wife got up as well and began to clear the table. "Don't worry, Oskar," she said to me, "everything will be alright. In the meantime I insist that you spend the night here with us."

I thanked her again for the meal and her hospitality. I stayed at the table to keep her company while she cleaned up the pots and the dishes. When she was finished she left the room and returned a short time later with a blanket and sheet for the couch. When she put them down she paused a moment before saying to me "If you like you may have a bath and get cleaned up." I was filthy, and she was clearly concerned for the condition of her blanket and couch.

"Of course! Again, thank you." I hadn't had a bath in weeks, even months, not since my capture. I'm sure that fact did not escape her.

When I finished my bath and walked back into the living room Nikolai had already returned. He nervously handed me a folded set of papers. I opened them and studied the writing carefully. The papers said that I was a Polish citizen and that I had been sent by the Germans to work in Russia. The document was signed on December nineteenth by Colonel Malinovski. Nikolai instructed me to bring them to the military recruiting center which was on the other side of the city. "Now go get some sleep," he said. "You should get an early morning start, but not too early so as to arouse suspicion."

I wished them good night as I settled on the couch to sleep. I was looking forward to this. Sleeping on a couch was another luxury that I had not been afforded in many months.

I stayed the night and got up early the next morning. I quietly left the house and headed toward Ulitza Moskravsk. Nikolai got up to see me off. As I left the house he told me not to mention that he saw me otherwise someone could trace the forged documents back to him. I nodded and thanked him again. I felt much safer now that I had papers with me, and walked openly through town and down the road to recruiting center. I held my head up while I walked, as if the papers I carried provided a shield that would keep away those who would do me harm. I arrived there around nine o'clock that morning. I discovered that center had become a large military installation similar to German military recruiting stations. Nikolai believed that if I were accepted into the Polish army there, they would bring me close to Kharkiv. It was time to put my plan into action.

Chapter 9   THE NKVD

     I walked into the center of the complex and located what I believed was the recruiting office. I confidently strolled inside. It wasn't long before someone noticed my arrival and approached me. I proudly presented the documents I carried to a major and announced that I was here to enlist in the Polish army. His face was expressionless while he thumbed through my papers. Without looking up at me he asked me a few general questions. I answered him directly, though I wasn't entirely truthful. When the exchange was done he picked his head up and held his gaze at me for a moment. Then he told me to take a seat. He watched as I sat in a nearby chair. He stayed at his desk and examined the documents a while longer. Then got up and instructed me to wait there for a few minutes. As he walked past me he, offered me a cigarette. I took one and thanked him. He paused to light it for me then left the room. It wasn't long before two different men came in carrying machineguns. They looked very much like NKVD officers. "Follow me" one of them said. I stood up without saying a word and waited for them to lead me on.

     The two guards escorted me back out the door and down the street to a large house where the NKVD was stationed. The place began to feel familiar to me. I had been here before during the time when my division occupied

Dnipropetrovs'k. I recognized the building that they brought me to. The Gestapo had used the house when the area was under German command.

The men led me into a small room and searched me. That was a clear indication that there was a problem. I tried to remain calm and put on the appearance that I had been expecting this treatment as normal. After they finished searching through my clothing, they brought me into another room to a different officer. Without a word the guard carrying my papers handed them to the officer. He acknowledged them and the two left the room. The officer briefly looked up at me then picked up the papers that Nikolai gave me and studied them critically. A minute later let them drop on to the desk before him, looked up and asked sternly "Did you create these papers yourself?"

"No, sir, I did not." I answered calmly. "How could I? I don't even know how to write in Russian."

"But you can speak in Russian?" he asked.

That was a mistake. A knot grew in my stomach. I looked at him, but gave him no reply.

"Where have you been?" he continued. "Where did you come from?"

"I came from right here in Dnipropetrovs'k. I am here to enlist in the Polish army."

With that he abruptly ended our conversation. His behavior seemed unusual, a sign that something was indeed terribly wrong. He pressed a button on his desk and soon one of the guards returned. The man took up a position behind me and pointed a machinegun at my back. The officer ordered the guard to take me to room ninety-eight. The man with the machinegun walked around me into view, glared at me and said, "Come along."

I stood up and followed him into a long hallway. As we walked through the corridor we passed by a few people who stared at me as I passed by. I was careful to look as casual as I could in an attempt to give the impression that I was totally innocent and this was just all a big mistake. When we arrived at room ninety-eight I saw a number of NKVD officials sitting around, including the major that I met earlier. One officer offered me a chair near him, and I sat down. The major asked me if I had something to eat this morning. I told him no. The man who offered me the chair left the room and a few minutes later returned with a small meal for me. He set before me a tray with some soup, a piece of bread, and some cheese. I glanced around the room and the officers were all looking at me and telling me "Eat, eat." They were watching my every move. Again I scanned the room in all directions. I knew exactly where I was; I was now under the jurisdiction of the GPU. We heard a lot about them during the war. It was a tense moment, and I put my faith in God for his help to get me through this. I thanked the man and ate the food that was placed before me in silence while the others watched. When I finished eating another man offered me a cigarette. I must say they were very polite.

We all knew what was coming next. They start off by cozying up to you with a meal and a cigarette, and then five minutes later comes the interrogation. Each of the officers in the room had a note pad. There was a scribe sitting to the right of the Major.

"What are your first and last names?"

"Oskar Scheja," I answered sternly.

"Born?"

"March fourth, 1908, in Krakau. I am presently living in Katowice with my parents."

The scribe recorded all of my answers. The officers wrote on their notepads, probably their own observations. Some of them pushed their notes in front of the major.

The major went on: "What are you doing here in Russia?"

"I worked for a German company in Dnipropetrovs'k. At the time the German troops retreated from the city I was far away from Dnipropetrovs'k in a small village. I do not know the name of the village."

Then one of the officers placed another sheet of paper in front of the major. I continued: "I want to get away from the Germans. I don't want to work for them any longer. One of the civilians I met in the village told me that as soon as the front moves through, I should enlist in the Polish army since I am a Polish citizen. I took that advice and left to come here. Two weeks went by and the Germans did make their retreat. The Germans left in the evening and the next morning the Russians were already there. I went to the Russian commander and he gave me the credentials that you have before you. He told me to bring them to the recruiting station in Dnipropetrovs'k. That's really all I can say."

A different officer asked: "Can you remember anything about the town you stayed in? Can you find it again if someone were to accompany you?"

I told him simply "I don't believe I could find it again."

He asked me "Do you have any acquaintances in Dnipropetrovs'k?"

"No," I replied, "I only came here to find work."

The men looked around at each other again. The officer asking me the questions continued writing in his note pad. When he was finished he looked at me and asked "Is everything you told me correct?"

"Yes, it is," I answered quickly.

"Then please sign here to attest to it." The officer removed the paper from his note pad and handed it to me. I quickly took the document from him, signed it, and handed it back.

Looking satisfied, he handed the paper to the major behind the desk. The major took the paper, gave it a quick look, and then called for an escort. It wasn't long before two men with machine guns entered the room. They walked behind me and ordered me to stand up and come with them. I casually complied. The three of us walked back down the hallway and out of the building. We marched down the street a short distance to the house next door. It had small, gated windows. It was no secret what lies in there.

As we entered the building, the men led me around the corner to a small room where a man was sitting behind a large desk. He was clearly the prison warden. The guards turned and left. The warden stared at me for a moment.

"Remove your suspenders and hand them to me" he said in a gruff voice. I silently complied.

He took the suspenders from me and placed them on the table. "Now empty your pockets and place everything on the desk."

I reached into my pockets and discovered that I still had with me half a slice of bread and a piece of dried bacon that Nikolai had given me for the trip. I also had two pair of gloves on me which I placed on the table, but the warden gestured to me that I may keep them.

"Turn out your pockets so that I may see that they are empty" he continued. "Now turn around."

He continued to study me from across the desk. Feeling satisfied he pulled himself up off the chair and said, "Come with me." I held my pants up with my hand as the warden led me down a long corridor. It was dark and cold. The silence was broken by our footsteps. On both sides there were iron doors with padlocks and a small flap that revealed a peep hole. When we reached the room that would become my cell, the warden took out a collection of keys and unlocked the door. As he opened the door, it made a loud noise that echoed down the corridor. The sound made me feel as though I was in an old church. The environment contrasted starkly from my previous incarceration, and part of me was very happy that I was being held in such a place. It appeared that I would at least be taken care of and that no one was going to shoot me.

I wondered for how long I would be held here but I did not have much time to think on it as I was distracted when the warden quickly ripped the gloves away from me, probably because he didn't have any himself. I was accustomed to treatment like that from the Russians. When you possessed something they wanted they decided that it no longer belonged to you, but instead to the State. Just then I was shoved in the back and I found myself in the middle a cell while the door closed behind me. I looked around the dimly lit room and saw four high walls, a small gated window, and seven men. They greeted me warmly, as one who would share their suffering.

At first I believed that the men who stood before me all looked very good, as their faces appeared full. It was a sign that I would be well cared for in this place. But I was wrong, as I then noticed that their stomachs were bloated from being undernourished. They were seven Russian civilians who were already convicted of one crime or another. They were happy to have the company of another and eager to speak with me. It wasn't long before I became friendly with them and learned about each one.

The first prisoner was an engineer who worked in a German factory. The second was the head of a dairy that provided butter, milk and cream to German military hospitals. The third was a mayor from a nearby town. The fourth was a manager of a railroad station in Dnipropetrovs'k. The fifth was a barber who had catered to German soldiers. The sixth was a man who worked for a company in Pavlograd that made sunflower seed oil. And the seventh was a police officer working for the Germans. The last one was the youngest at age twenty-one. He was very funny and spoke good German. Throughout my incarceration he would sing to me over and over again the song "Ich bin der Bub vom Fuldatal" (I am the kid from Fuldatal).

The youngest one received the longest sentence, twenty years in Siberia. The engineer, the railroad station manager, and the head of the dairy all received sentences of fifteen years in Siberia. Two had ten years and one had seven. I was still waiting for my sentence.

The temperature in the room was a chilly four degrees Celsius. There was no stove to provide warmth. The floor was made of dark stone. There were no benches or furnishings of any kind. The only object in the room other than the eight of us was a large pail for everyone to use as our toilet. There was no air circulation at all, and the stench from the pail and the men who probably hadn't bathed in weeks or even months was terrible. As the day went on, we talked quietly together. Each of them was happy to have a newcomer with whom they could share their experience. They were eager to learn about my background, but I avoided conversation about me. I revealed only that I was a Polish citizen trying to enlist in the Polish army, and that I did not know why I was being detained here.

The day dragged on. When we got cold we paced from one corner to another to get warm. When night fell we huddled together for warmth, looking like a family of rats in a nest. And the lice! We didn't have lice, the lice had us.

Early the next morning at six o'clock we were woken by the warden and we each took turns using the pail. I learned that meals were only served once a day at two o'clock in the afternoon. Each received 250 grams of bread and a half liter of potato water. That was our entire ration for the whole day.

Night fell again and a second day passed in the cell. The conversations were fewer. Eventually the Russians figured out that I would not tell them much about me at all and they stopped asking. They would talk amongst themselves from time to time, telling stories of their experiences during the war and even laughing about them. Though they were clearly suffering, they seemed to find a measure of peace in each other's company. I admired them for that.

More often than not it was very quiet in the jail, but above all it was very cold. From time to time one of us would pace the cell back and forth. A third day came and went. There was still no word on what would become of me. After four days I noticed that I was growing weaker. It was becoming more difficult to get up off the floor. A week went by, then another. After fifteen days I started to look bloated, just like the others.

Finally I reached my breaking point and I couldn't take it any longer. With great effort I banged on the door to get the warden's attention. After a moment, I heard someone's footsteps come down the hall and stop in front of our cell. A man opened the flap and bellowed, "What do you want?"

"I want to speak to the person in charge." I said weakly.

The man chuckled, and without a word closed the flap and walked slowly back down the hallway. A few minutes later the man returned. He fumbled for the key but eventually unlocked the door and swung it open. "Come with me," he said.

I followed the man down the hall until I came upon the warden. He was the guy who took my gloves.

"Sir," I explained, breathing heavy as I labored for every word, "I am a Polish citizen. I came here to this station in order to enlist in the army. When I arrived here I was locked up. I don't even know why I'm here. Can you please tell me what is going on?"

He held up the documents that were sent with me by the NKVD and casually looked through them. He put them aside and said "You must be patient. It takes a long time to complete the paperwork."

"Paperwork for what?" I asked.

He looked down at his desk and sighed. "Follow me," he said. He brought me to the next room where there was a major sitting. He laid my paperwork in front of the major and the warden said to him in Russian "We'll send this dog to Siberia for ten years."

I understood what he said to the Major and asked him, "What for? I didn't do anything!"

The major looked at me smugly, gave me a thumbs down sign and said, "It matters not. No one comes into Russia. You will go back to where you belong." The thumbs down sign meant that I would never see home again.

I could think of nothing more to say in my defense. The warden led me out and brought me back to the prison guard, who in turn locked me back in the cell. My other cell mates approached me and quickly asked me what the major and the warden said to me. I gave them a short answer and made it clear that I did not want to discuss it. There was no point in sharing any information with them, as they could not help me.

From December twentieth until the eighth of January I was held in this house. We spent Christmas and New Years there, but we did not think about the holidays.

Then early in the morning on January eighth the warden came to wake us, but this time he unlocked the door and called my name.

"Yes," I replied.

"Come with me."

I sensed that I would not return to this cell, so I said good-bye to my fellow suffering prison mates. I was sad to leave them in a way. I was struck by how positive they remained, despite the deplorable conditions we shared. They had such a cheerful look on their faces as they said their good-byes to me as well. One of them called out to me to say that we'll see each other again on the transport to Siberia, as if he were looking forward to sharing the ride with me. When the warden heard that he laughed. I followed him back to the reception area an officer was waiting for me along with three guards armed with machine guns. Each of the guards had a pack strapped to his back loaded with provisions. I knew that I'd be leaving this place and wondered where they were taking me. The officer took my papers and scanned them quickly. He looked up at me and asked sternly "Do you speak Russian?" I answered simply, "Yes".

"Good. Now listen to me very carefully. Do not do anything stupid underway. If you take one step out of line, to the left or the right, these three men will shoot you. Do you understand?" "Yes" I replied. It was clear that my situation was not going to improve.

The officer folded my papers and handed them to one of the guards. Without a word he gestured to me to come with him. They led me out of the jail through the streets toward the middle of town. The roads were very crowded. People looked at me wide-eyed and wondered what kind of criminal I was, guarded by three men with machine guns. It left me feeling cold. Before long we arrived at the train station, where I faced even larger crowds staring at me. By the time I got there, I was tired and out of breath. The lack of food had taken quite a toll on my body, but the guards would not let me rest just yet. They shoved me along until we reached the train platform. I tried to sit on the ground to wait for the train, but with guns pointed at me they ordered me to remain standing. About twenty minutes later, the train arrived and we boarded. The guards directed me to a compartment where I finally had a chance to sit. On the left side of me, there was a window. The guard watching me sat in the corner, and the other two on another bench. The lieutenant ordered me to go to sleep. I laughed to myself at the thought that I could be ordered to go to sleep.

It was ten minutes after eleven when the train left the station. The sign on the platform said that we were headed towards Kharkiv-Moscow. I rested against the wall and closed my eyes.

It was a long train ride through vast stretches of snow-covered fields. I felt the emptiness of the landscape as my hopes dimmed for a positive outcome. I became aware that the other people in the train car were very curious about me. They asked the lieutenant if I were a Russian. He answered again and again that he's a Fritz pretending to be a Pole. I understood every conversation the officer had. I realized there was no way I was getting out of here, where ever this train was taking me.

At three o'clock in the morning, we arrived in Kharkiv. We waited for the other passengers to exit the train before the guards escorted me off. We walked through the train station and a short distance into the town center until we arrived at a building that was the NKVD office. The lieutenant brought my papers to one of the officers, and I was told to sit and wait to receive further instructions. A few hours later, the Lieutenant came back and ordered me to get up. My guards and I marched back to the train station. This time we got on board a train heading south. We traveled for two days and two nights before we arrived at our destination. When the train came to a halt we were at a stop that had no markings to indicate where I was. I listened carefully as the guards talked among themselves. I learned that our destination was a place that was about twenty-three kilometers south of Stalino. The Lieutenant looked at me and in a mocking tone told me that in an hour from now I would be back home. To get there, we had to walk about four kilometers.

Chapter 10 CAMP 240

We stepped off the train at small station that
appeared to be hastily erected in the middle of nowhere. The
weather was terrible. We were in the middle of a big
snowstorm and a deep freeze. I was chilled to the bone
because I had very little left on my bones to keep me warm.
Without delay we began to trudge through the deepening
snow. The guards mocked me and stuck the barrel of their
guns in my back to keep me moving. Off in the distance
through the driving snow and sheets of ice rain, an outline of
what appeared to be a large prison camp came into view. It
was no surprise to me that I would end up in a place such as
this.

As we got closer, we heard an unexpected noise
through the wind-swept snow. It was the sound of people
singing. It was a very sad song. I expected a German
melody, but as I got closer and heard the singing more
clearly I was surprised to discover that it was not German.
The people were instead singing in Russian. Further along
the path we encountered the long column of people marching
away from the camp toward the direction we came from.
It's likely their destination was the same small train station.
It reminded me of a movie I saw back home where the men
were banished to Siberia as punishment. As we passed by
them, the prisoners hardly acknowledged our existence while
they plodded through the storm. A profound sadness

gripped me. The Lieutenant sensed this and took the opportunity to assert his authority over me. He pointed at the column of men and said, "See, those are your fellow sufferers. Welcome home." The other guards chuckled.

The prison was called "NKVD Camp 240". It was a place not for German war prisoners, but instead for enemies of the State. The camp was encircled by five rolls of barbed wire. On the corners, there were machine gun towers. Every fifty meters there was an armed guard, and every hundred meters a watchdog. There were fifteen thousand prisoners in the camp made up of people from all walks of life. Some were high-ranking officials, but most were insignificant workers. The prisoner population included about eight hundred women. The people held in this camp were mostly Russian civilians found guilty of collaborating with the enemy, by working in German manufacturing companies. There were also military officers here who had been captured by the German army and later released to work for the Germans. They were used here in the camp as spies.

I arrived at the camp on January eleventh, 1944. The guards brought me to a building near the camp entrance, handed over my papers to a waiting attendant. They quickly forgot about me as they left my side to warm themselves and converse with the camp guards. A man behind a large desk processed me very quickly, as if he had done this a thousand times. There was no doubt in my mind that he had. He gestured to one of the men that his work was finished. The guard that he pointed to seemed a bit annoyed to taken away from his conversation with the soldiers and hastily grabbed me by the arm to bring me to my next destination. It was a barrack that was full of men who were recently brought here.

There were two such barracks where the new prisoners were kept. We were required to remain there in quarantine as a safeguard against carrying epidemics and sicknesses into the camp.

The prison hierarchy was structured by company, then battalion, and then by group. Each had its leader. I learned that I was assigned to the fifth Karmatin Company, second battalion, sixth group. The battalion leader met me at the door, then escorted me into the barrack. His battalion was spread out over three rooms. Each room was only about four meters by four meters, yet housed one hundred and seven men.

I walked inside and the sight of the appalling conditions stopped me dead in my tracks. The battalion leader followed me in, closed the door behind me, turned to me and mechanically recited the following instructions: "Order and discipline will rule here. The wakeup call is at five o'clock. At seven o'clock you will receive one liter of soup as ration. At eight o'clock the barracks will be cleaned. At twelve o'clock you will receive six hundred grams of bread, one hundred grams of fish, and twenty-five grams of sugar. At four o'clock there will be more soup, and at six o'clock it is time for sleeping. You are not required to do any work while in quarantine. Your orders are only to stay put in these barracks for the next twenty-one days and not cause any trouble. Do you understand?"

Without looking up at him I simply replied "Yes".

He turned and left me standing there. I took a deep breath and walked into one of the rooms and tried my best to ignore the faces staring at me, as I forced my through the mass of bodies to an open spot on the wall. When I reached the edge of the room, I sunk down to the floor with my knees folded up to my chest. I was overcome with immense sadness. The conditions were intolerable. Outside it was a chilly, below zero Celsius, but by contrast you could die in the rooms from the heat and foul air. It was dark outside and all I wanted to do was to close my eyes and hide. I sat expressionless on the floor, too exhausted to think. Two hours later it was lights-out and time to sleep, but we were packed so tightly together in the room that at night it was impossible to sleep with your legs stretched out. We practically slept on top of each other. There was a foot in my back. Each time I bumped up against the man behind me he shoved me away. I was too tired and sad to care. It was the worst night of my life.

The next morning when the first meal was served I soon discovered that we never received the correct amount of rations promised to us. That's because the Russian commanders received the same food as the prison inmates. They were served first, starting with the company leader. He took what he wanted and gave the rest to the battalion leaders. Each battalion leader received the rations for his battalion. Each would take what he wanted to fill his belly and distribute the rest to the group leaders. When each group leaders received his rations to distribute the same thing was at work. So from the six hundred kilograms of bread we were promised we only received about four hundred grams. Out of a hundred grams of fish there were only sixty, and there was no twenty-five grams of sugar but instead about ten.

It was pointless to complain. When the men gathered around the food distribution point, I took advantage of the vacated space and found myself an inconspicuous corner where I didn't have to interact with anyone. The bread distribution finally reached me. I asked a fellow prisoner to bring me my soup. He was very happy to do it because it benefited him. When he returned, it was obvious that he took his cut as well. There was only about a half of liter of soup left for me. I turned my back to the room and ate my share very slowly. I used this as a task to focus my attention away from the discomfort and sadness that enveloped me. When I was finished, there was nothing more to do than to sink back into my despair.

I spent each miserable day trying my best to avoid contact with everyone. I knew that the inmates in the room were curious about me because I rarely spoke. Escape from the camp was impossible. On the fourth day a prison guard walked past me while I sat on the floor and took a liking to the boots I was wearing. He ordered me to remove them. I had no choice but to comply, and without a word I handed them to the guard. He held them up to inspect them and removed one of his shoes to try them on, then the other. Satisfied with his new prize he tossed his old, torn shoes at my face and walked away. I gathered them and casually put them on my feet as if I were expecting this.

Two days later, the temperature in the rooms began to drop. We had run out of our allotment of coal for the fire. We were told that we were responsible for burning too much coal too quickly and would have to do without until our next ration came. Of course the officers remained warm. A small measure of heat from those rooms would make its way down the hall and reach the rooms where the prisoners were kept. A spot near the door became highly prized and was the source of several arguments. I was content to remain in my corner. I tried to make myself as small as possible to preserve as much of my body heat as I could, but it was no use. The wall was like ice. Though my coat was thick, it would not provide enough insulation from the cold. Nor could I escape the stench. I thought that eventually I would grow accustomed to the foul odor of the room, but I never did.

I suffered from an indescribable hunger and an intolerable chill. Of all the hardships I had endured during the war, I had never felt such misery. Every day I felt weaker and more alone. I could think of nothing else but desolation and despair. I am sure that my family, friends, and battalion mates from the army had presumed long ago that I was dead. I may as well be.

I held out for fourteen days, at which point I decided that I couldn't take any more of it. I had reached the limit of my despair. I felt that the only option they left open for me was to take my own life.

That decision alone provided me with a measure of comfort that I had not experienced in some time. At least I had a purpose, a goal to achieve other than just enduring each miserable day. I set about to prepare myself for the task. I found a spot in the room where I could keep an eye on the guards' quarters. I waited until all of the guards had left their rooms and I was safely out of their sight. When no one was looking, I quickly stepped in to their quarters and took a razor blade left by the sink. I would use it so slit my wrists. I tucked it into the sleeve of my coat and casually walked back out. I returned to my corner of the room with my prize and sat on the floor. I slowly took the blade out of my pocket, careful to make sure no one could see what I was doing, and stared at it for a long while.

I turned the blade over in my hands a few times. I grew excited that my suffering would soon be at an end. I assumed that my thoughts would turn to my loved ones that I would leave behind, my family and friends, but instead I couldn't stop thinking of the Russians I met in the NKVD prison cell at the recruiting center. They faced their adversity with such grace. I admired them for that and felt ashamed that I could not do the same. What weakness runs through me that does not inhabit their bodies? My excitement turned to confusion. I was allowing myself to be defeated. Suddenly in my mind I was back digging through the rock-hard earth to construct the trenches around Kharkiv as we prepared to capture the city. "Every resistance can be broken." That's what our training taught us. Was I not working hard enough to break this resistance? Or was it the other way around, that the Russians finally broke my resistance? A moment ago, I had such clarity when I made the decision to end my life. I grew frustrated now that I had lost that focus. I kept turning the blade over in my hands while I studied it. I believed it would help me re-gain my sense of purpose.

But in an instant everything changed. Looking back at it now, I believe it was nothing short of a miracle.

I was unaware that one of the prisoners took notice of me and understood what I was planning to do. He quietly walked away and found the battalion commander. I kept my back to the room while I studied the blade, but after a few minutes I felt the presence of people standing very close to me. I slowly turned around and looked up in horror to see two men staring down at me. A tear streaked down my face. The commander ordered me to stand up. I slipped the blade back into the sleeve of my coat and obeyed, struggling to get on my fee.

"Who are you? What is your name?" asked the commander. His voice was gentle but firm.

"My name is Oskar Scheja. I am a Pole. I don't know why I'm here. I shouldn't be here." My voice cracked. I was so weak and upset that it was hard to think. I labored over every word and found myself taking long pauses between sentences. "I was an officer in the Polish army. My only crime is that I wanted to re-join the Polish army. That is all. That is all I wanted to do. I just wanted to get back to the army. Instead they brought me to this place. I don't know what I've done to deserve this. Look at me. I don't know. I don't …" I tried hard to hold back my tears, but in the middle of my explanation I simply gave up. They had broken me, and I didn't care what this man thought of me.

The commander paused. I felt him look me over though I did not look up at him. I kept my eyes fixed on the ground. I waited for him to decide what to do with me, this pathetic wretch under his watch. He took a deep breath and asked "Are you receiving your rations?"

"Yes" I replied.

"That's not true!" said the prisoner who reported me, taking interest in the drama. "I see him. He's one of the people who never receive anything, but he is too shy to tell anyone about it."

I picked my head up to see how he would react to this. Why would he care? I was effectively sent here to die anyway. The commander looked me up and down and I could sense a reaction that I did not expect. He seemed to take pity on me. He glanced over his shoulder and sent for his comrade, a lieutenant Anitschenko who was from Kiev.

Anitschenko came into the room, approached us and said "Yes, commander."

"Take this man to the bath house and get him cleaned up and de-loused."

"Yes, sir." Anitschenko responded. "Here, come with me." He started to lead me out of the barracks, but the commander called him back for more instructions, leaving me near the door as I leaned against the wall to steady myself. Though I did not hear the conversation, I learned that he also gave the lieutenant orders to get me some new clothes. On our way to the bath house, Anitschenko took a pair off officer's boots away from one of the other guards. He also found a pair of pants, a green German shirt, and a civilian coat that was still in good shape. It was a long, black fur coat, similar to the one I had before, but in much better condition. He handed them all to me. Although I did not speak I looked up and gave him a sincere smile to show him my gratitude. I could see that made him happy.

I was so weak from hunger that I could barely stand. Lieutenant Anitschenko steadied me and helped me get dressed in the bath house. As we started to remove my shabby clothing the razor blade slipped out of my sleeve and fell to the floor, making a soft clang that broke the silence. We both paused for a moment looking down at the shiny object. Looking down at it made me feel ashamed. I tried to reach for it to quickly put it out of my sight, but as I stretched my arm out I nearly fell over. Anitschenko quickly steadied me with one arm and with the other reached down and calmly picked up the blade. As he stood, he slipped it into his coat pocked, turned to me and said "You will not need this any longer, unless of course you wish to shave." He sensed that I was uncomfortable speaking about it and we focused again on getting me cleaned up. Though our conversation ended, he was patient and kind. It took me a long time to get cleaned up and dressed, as I was moving rather slowly. The Lieutenant didn't seem to mind at all. Perhaps he was happy to be doing something other than maintaining discipline and order. When I was finally ready, he escorted me back to the battalion commander who greeted me with a friendly smile.

"There. You look much better now, Oskar Scheja."

"Yes. Yes, I do. Thank you, commander."

"Come with me" he ordered, and I obediently followed. The commander introduced me to the other officers in the battalion. Among them was a Jew, Captain Tarrakanov, also from Kiev. They were all happy to meet me, standing up to give me their hand as they were introduced. I was unaccustomed to treatment like this from the officers and it made me feel uncomfortable. Then Anitschenko told me to follow him back out of the barracks. We walked a short distance to a building that housed the camp leaders. Anitschenko introduced me to several of the leaders and other guards who were in the building. One of them was a man named Stolleruck, who was from Stalino. I was puzzled by all the attention I was receiving, but it certainly changed my mood so I just went along without thinking too much more about it. Back in my own barracks while Anitschenko was doing this, the commander was at work discussing my situation with his superiors.

When we were finished with my introductions we returned to the barracks. Anitschenko brought me into one of the guard rooms where the commander was waiting for me. He asked me to take a seat.

"I reviewed your file, Oskar. Is it all true, that you were indeed an officer in the Polish army?"

"Yes, commander."

"And the papers you carried with you were not forged?"

"No, commander. I was truthful about everything."

The commander looked over at Anitschenko who gave him a faint nod.

"Oskar," the commander continued, "we believe that you were too hastily placed here. We have good relations with the Polish army now. Unfortunately, that fact is that I cannot release you from this camp."

I looked down to the floor and replied, "I understand."

"But I can help you. The war is turning in our favor. We have the Germans on the run. As you know, we lost many soldiers in the war, but more are needed to chase the invaders back to Berlin and secure our victory. We are very short on guards in this camp. If you are indeed a former officer of the Polish army, then I am willing to accept you into the tenth company as one of the officers."

I slowly looked up at the commander in disbelief. I realized quickly that I needed to remove the look of shock on my face in order not to arouse suspicion that their decision was not appropriate. Still, I could hardly contain my emotions. My voice quivered slightly as I answered softly, "You what?"

"Lieutenant Anitschenko will get you situated. Congratulations, Oskar."

With that the commander stood up and left the room. I tried to stand up as well, but had trouble doing it quickly enough to be upright before he had already vanished from view. Anitschenko supported my arm, helping me to my feet.

I looked at Anitschenko. "I don't know what to say. I ..." I could speak no more as I diverted my energy to holding back my tears.

"Come," he said, "there are more people you need to meet. Then I will bring you to your quarters and you can rest for a while."

The commander led me into the company staff room. There he introduced me to a Lieutenant Nikolai Scharappil from Moscow, who was an Aide-de-Camp in a regiment that was guarding a number of partisan inmates. I thought I must look pathetic to him, but he was accustomed to seeing men in my condition and paid no mind to having an officer that could barely get himself dressed. They assigned me quarters in the room and gave me a job to help the company with the battalion orders. They even provided me with a uniform. I was clearly tired and overwhelmed by the events of the past hour. Lieutenant Scharappil ordered me to my quarters to rest until the evening meal was served. I happily obliged.

For the first time in weeks I was able to lie down with my legs and torso completely stretched out. The room was warm, as there was plenty of coal in the fire, and I was curled up in my beautiful, new black fur coat. I was overwhelmed with the feeling of being comfortable. It was a remarkable sensation. The emptiness in my stomach was not yet stilled, but I took solace from knowing that I would soon have a fulfilling portion of food. I was still in shock over how quickly my fortunes had changed. Within hours I went from being a prisoner suffering from starvation and about to take his own life, to an officer working with the Russian army. Imagine me, an officer in the Russian ranks! How did I manage to pull that off? I was proud of myself and smiled. I also had to acknowledge the kindness shown by my Russian captors, my enemies. It was yet another thing I was not expecting. "How strange," I said aloud.

A few hours later I awoke from a brief sleep to accept my evening rations. For the first time in many months, I was able to eat enough to fully satisfy my hunger. My stomach was not accustomed to eating much food and so it took me several days before I could eat normally. Anitschenko excused me for the rest of the evening. I gratefully retired to my bunk, but I knew that I had much work to do. It was one thing to pull off this deception, but that was only the beginning. I was not out of danger. I needed to remain here in this position until an opportunity arose to indeed get back to the Polish army, and ultimately back to the German army, or to some other circumstance where I was truly safe. I wanted to get back on my feet and work hard to earn their trust and confidence. That was my new purpose. It was far different than the goal I had previously chosen for myself just a few hours earlier.

The next morning I arose and got myself dressed. Anitschenko came into my room to get me and smiled when he saw me in my new uniform. It took a great deal of effort, but I made it through the first day, carrying out every order given to me punctually and efficiently. As each day passed, the rations were becoming a bit larger and I started to feel more human. In addition, I received one hundred grams of tobacco every ten days, the same amount that the Russian officers received. After a short time, I was beginning to get my strength back. Fourteen days after being accepted in the battalion the commander promoted me to dispatcher. I have to say again and again that I was so grateful that God had not forsaken me.

Chapter 11 SPIES

It had been four weeks since my acceptance into the Russian military. I was still very much elated by this strange twist of fate, but the pleasure I took from that had started to wane. I was by no means out of danger. My battalion leader was promoted from penal commander to storm commander and called up to the front line. Captain Tarrakanov of the tenth company took over as platoon leader. I was still regarded as a "Porutshnik", a first lieutenant, though many of my fellow prison guards were saying that I should have been ranked higher.

I found the Russian prisoners to be very curious about everyone in camp. I would often hear them gossip and whisper about other inmates and officers. I suppose there wasn't much more to do during the day to keep the men occupied, but it seemed to be a natural Russian trait to learn everything you could about everyone you meet.

One evening after our rations had been distributed I met up with Captain Tarrakanov and two other officers from our platoon in the captain's quarters. I was feeling much better and had just finished the evening meal. The room was warm and the prisoners were quiet in their barracks. I forgot for a while that I was still in the company of my enemies in a prison camp, and instead allowed myself to enjoy a smoke and a pleasant conversation with people I was beginning to call my friends. I was getting along well with my fellow officers, but always careful to tell them as little about me as possible.

At one point Tarrakanov noticed that I wasn't saying very much, and turned to me to include me in the conversation. "You know Oskar, the men in the barracks are talking about you."

"Oh?" I replied simply. I didn't like where this conversation was going, but went along with it.

"Yes. I hear it all the time. They say 'Who is this guy? He can't be a Russian.'"

I took another drag on my cigarette and smiled.

Tarrakanov continued: "When you walk by I hear the men say, 'There goes the man in the black fur coat.' That's what they call you, you know, 'the man in the black fur coat'."

"Yes, I hear that, too." I took another puff and offered no more. There was a long pause in the conversation before one of the other officers began to tell a story about the inmates. I was relieved that the attention turned away from me. I casually listened, but became lost in my own thoughts. I did hear that a lot from the men: "There goes the man in the black fur coat." That's pretty much all I let them learn about me. And so I became known around the camp simply as "the man in the black fur coat". Some would stop me and ask questions of me directly, but I would give each one a different answer. I would tell one person that I was a Frenchman, to another I was an Englishman, and the next person a Pole. In the end, no one had a clue who I really was.

It was a dangerous game that I was playing, but it was also exiting. I had to be extremely careful not reveal to anyone who I was, not the guards or the prisoners. I wondered for how long I could keep this up. Of course, I knew it wasn't a game. This was real, and my life depended on it.

A similar conversation repeated nearly every evening. Lieutenant Scharappil would tell us stories about what the men were saying about me. Some said I was an Englishman, a Frenchman, a Pole, and a few doubted all of those things and believed I could just as well be a German. I enjoyed the mystery I had created and felt quite proud of myself.

Each day I would go for a walk through the camp with Lieutenants Anitschenko and Scharappil. We always made sure to walk past the area where the women were housed. There were a few that we were quite fond of, and two in particular that I was attracted to. I knew, of course, that getting very close to anyone in this place would be foolish. I was still in a prison camp of the G.P.U. I remained disciplined and pushed those feelings aside. One afternoon while we were in our officers' quarters Lieutenant Anitschenko said to me "Oskar, let's take a walk again after dinner. There is someone new who recently arrived in the camp. She is a first lieutenant in the army. She comes directly from the front line to observe the operation here. She saw you and I together yesterday evening and she asked me about you. I think she likes you. She asked me if we could meet with her tonight and I promised her I would arrange that."

I had become good friends with the company leader, Captain Tarrakanov. He overheard my conversation with Anitschenko. Later, when Anitschenko left, Tarrakanov approached me. He looked me in the eye and said "Just between the two of us, Oskar, you know about the G.P.U. You need to be careful."

"Yes, I know what you're saying." I patted him on the knee. "Thank you for looking out for me."

Later that evening Anitschenko came by my quarters. "Oskar!" he barked to get my attention. I looked up at him without saying a word. He gestured to me that I should follow him, as it was time for our walk. I grabbed my coat and accompanied him out of the door. We walked a short distance to the women's barracks, saying very little to each other along the way. As we got to the door, he smiled at me and said "You'll like her." I thought about the advice that Tarrakanov gave to me. I hoped that I wasn't about do to something stupid, but I was curious and did not want to disappoint Anitschenko. He seemed to have gone through great lengths to arrange this meeting as a nice gesture to me. I needed to show my gratitude.

As we got to the barracks, he rapped on the door. I saw a figure come to the window, disappear for a moment, then emerge from the building. Her name was Anna and she was strikingly beautiful. She stood one hundred and seventy centimeters tall, blonde and full-figured. It has been a long time since I last gazed upon a woman like her. In an instant I decided I made the right decision to put aside Tarrakanov's warning. She took a few steps out to join us. Anitschenko introduced her to me: "Anna, this is Oskar."

"Hello, Oskar," she said warmly as she held out her hand.

I casually replied "Hello," as I reached to take her hand and gently held it for a moment. She wore a new, full length coat, a fur cap, and a white scarf, but no gloves. Her skin was cold but soft, and I was careful not clasp her delicate hand too tightly as we made brief eye contact. The three of us promptly turned away from the building and began our stroll around the camp grounds. Anitschenko and Anna engaged in some light conversation as we walked between the dark buildings. Bright lights illuminated the fence that encircled the grounds, but the pathways were dark. You could see the guards in the towers turn their attention to us from time to time. After a few minutes, Anna turned to bring me into the conversation.

"So, Oskar, you're new in camp?"

"Yes. I arrived in January."

We walked a few more steps she added, "And I heard that you're a Polish officer?"

"That is correct" I replied. I did not look at her when I spoke. I tried to keep my answers short and not offer too much.

Anna seemed determine to strike up a conversation with me. Anitschenko remained quiet, as if he did his job and now waited for his desired result to emerge. Although she was very pleasant, I also understood she could be just as dangerous for me.

"Do you speak German, Oskar?" she asked.

I was waiting for a question like that. I felt a rush of relief that my apprehension about the encounter was warranted. I was now able to continue the conversation at ease, knowing exactly what was going on here and I was now in complete control. I paused before answering in German, "Yes, a little bit, but not very well."

She was proud to tell me that she could speak it fluently and proceeded to converse with me only in German. I answered her in broken German phrases, careful to make some grammatical mistakes, but not sound obvious that I was faking it. I did not answer any questions right away, giving the impression that I needed to first assemble the German phrase in my mind before I could get it out. I asked how she had come to this camp and in great detail she explained that she was sent here for observation. The three of us talked for a while until the evening was over, as at ten o'clock everyone needed to be in their barrack. When it was time to part ways, she asked me if we could meet again tomorrow night and I agreed. Anitschenko explained that he was unable to come, so it would be just the two of us.

Anitschenko and I walked the short distance back to our barracks. "Well, Oskar," he remarked, "Was I right?"

I looked at him and smiled. "Yes, she is quite lovely."

"Ha!" he blurted out, then blew on his hands to warm them up. "Yes. Yes, she is."

We walked the rest of the way in silence and said 'good night' to each other as I turned to enter my quarters. I quickly made myself comfortable in my bed to think about the encounter. I wondered where this would take me.

I met Anna the following evening at her barracks in the same manner only this time I was alone with her. We hastily began our walk without the pleasantries that we exchanged when we greeted each other the day before. She continued to speak to me only in German, but this time had very little to say. She directed our walk away from the well-lit perimeter and instead we meandered on the dimly-lit walkways between the barracks. She acted as if she were quite distracted by something. I asked her what was on her mind.

"Oskar," she began, "I have been thinking all night and day about something." I remained silent while we walked, patiently waiting for her to continue. "I was wondering how someone could escape from this camp."

I still offered no reply. I thought I'd keep her hanging for a bit to see how she would continue. It was my way of making it clear that I was in control here.

She nervously continued. "I'm sure the prisoners in this camp think about it all the time. So what do they think about? What kind of plans would they make? It must always be on their minds and they have all day to think on it. I'm certain that some have identified a weakness."

I shrugged and said, "I wouldn't know."

Our footsteps echoed off of the walls of the buildings as we walked. It was very quiet, adding an uneasy feeling to the direction of this conversation. We came to a dark corner of a storage building where there were no windows. She stopped walking and turned to me.

"Would you join me?"

I looked at her quizzically. "Would I what?"

She whispered back "Would you escape with me? Together."

I certainly didn't expect that question, but I was beginning to understand what was at work here. "I would consider it. Yes. So you have found a way out of here? How?"

"Yes, and I know it will work. Every morning at nine o'clock a truck arrives carrying food and supplies to the stock house. The driver always rides alone. He is an acquaintance of mine from my homeland. He always takes along some empty barrels. We could climb into the truck and hide in them. Once we are out of the camp we could make our way to the Caucasus where my parents live. Once we are there I would take care of everything else."

I listened carefully to everything she had to say. She waited nervously for my reaction. After an intentionally uncomfortable period of silence responded, "That sounds good. It's clever."

She was happy that I seemed to approve and she smiled. "It will work, I know it will."

"But why would you want to leave this camp?" Before she could answer I continued, "I do like it here. But I know of a different camp in Moscow that is much nicer. The accommodations are a hundred percent better." I looked her in the eye and added, "And I have heard that you can even get married there."

Her expression changed and she looked at me quite startled. I smiled back at her. Though I spoke in broken German, I believed she understood me.

"That sounds good." she said, as we began to walk again. From that moment Anna became much less talkative. We returned to her barracks as the evening ended quickly. She explained that she suddenly became very tired. We said good-bye and I asked when we could meet again. She didn't answer as she closed the door behind her. I smiled to myself as I turned to make the short walk back to my quarters, feeling quite proud of how I handled the situation.

The next day she vanished from the camp without a trace. I never saw her again.

Anna wasn't the last mysterious officer that I met in this camp. There were many others like her whom Captain Tarrakanov had warned me about. Just a few days later another woman started to make my acquaintance. She was different, or perhaps I saw her differently now that I was familiar with this game. It was obvious from the moment I met her that she was no prisoner. She was a little perp working for the G.P.U. I was sure of it. She approached me one afternoon while I was outside and struck up a conversation. "How's it going?"

"Good. And how are you?"

"Fine, thank you." She came a little closer and began to speak quietly. "Do you remember the blonde you met a few days ago?"

"Yes."

"Well, she is from the NKVD. She was ordered to find out more about you. However, when she couldn't get you to give up anything, she left and went back to her office."

I acted casual and unconcerned. I looked away from her toward the open camp grounds and asked "Why are you telling me this if you are also working with the NKVD?"

She leaned in to me and said softly "If I tell you, will you promise to keep this between us? I do not wish to end up a permanent fixture in this camp like you are."

"I promise."

"Alright, Oskar. If you really do wish to leave this camp, you should make a formal request of the NKVD in writing, stating that you are a Polish officer. The NKVD will consider your request and it may be possible for you to indeed return to the Polish army, if that is what you want."

Without another word from either of us, she turned and left.

I stood there alone for a moment in silent reflection. It was an interesting idea. Of course I didn't trust her as far as I could throw, her but nonetheless I decided there was no harm in giving it a try. It was the NKVD who landed me in this place and oddly enough they may also be the key to getting me out. I asked my good friend Captain Tarrakanov if he would write this request for me and he was happy to oblige. Tarrakanov, Anitschenko, Stolleruck, and Nikolai Scharappil all contributed by providing character references. Tarrakanov submitted the paperwork and I waited. Eventually my request made its way to the NKVD leaders and they asked me to come forward to offer some statements. When I was finished a captain in the NKVD told me to have patience while the papers were being sent to the headquarters in Moscow. He said that the couriers usually take a long time with these matters. So I waited.

One afternoon there was a commotion in the officer's company. I paid no mind to it until I heard Captain Tarrakanov booming voice call out to me, "Oskar! There's a countryman of yours here to see you." I was startled when I heard this, struck with fear that perhaps my charade was finally coming to an end. Had they discovered my true identify? I composed myself and strode casually into the officer's room and saw an unfamiliar face.

His name was Bruno Schmagelski. He was thirty-four years old and came from Kruschwitz, which is in the Danzig region of Poland. He was short, dirty, and malnourished like nearly all of the others here in camp, but he had a cheerful face that exposed a mischievous air about him. I learned that he lived in Kruschwitz until 1933 when he left Poland to settle in Germany near the city of Potsdam. There he had enlisted with the S.S. and ultimately came into the German Gestapo during the Polish campaign. After the campaign in Poland, he deserted the Gestapo and made his way into Russia. He was able to get around very well because he was fluent in both Russian and Polish, but more so because he was clever and resourceful. He settled in

Dnipropetrovs'k where he tried to stay inconspicuous, waiting for the time and the opportunity to get back to a Poland that he hoped would be free from the German army. Unfortunately, he raised enough suspicions with the locals that he was captured and held by Partisans operating in Dnipropetrovs'k who believed he was a spy. Bruno was able to convince them otherwise and they released him after only three days. He left Dnipropetrovs'k and traveled through Kharkiv in an attempt to reach Lemberg. There he hoped to return to civilian duties and blend in with the population but was taken into custody in Kharkiv by the NKVD. There he spent half a year in jail because he didn't have papers or credentials. From there, he was taken to this NKVD camp. He made it through the twenty-one days of quarantine and on April fifteenth, 1944 was assigned to the tenth company.

Here's where our paths merge: Since he entered the camp, he led on to the officers that he was in fact an ensign in the Polish army and wished only to return to the army.

Five officers accompanied Bruno into the room. One of the officers had a sack half full of dried bread and bacon, which he claimed a woman from the stockade had given to him. The officer who brought the sack with the food slept with it the entire night clenched in his hands for fear that someone would take it from him. But Bruno was a savvy thief. He got a hold of a razor blade, crept up to the officer while he slept, slit open the sack, and stole much of the food inside. When the officer woke up and felt the now half-empty sack in his hand he was enraged. He gathered a few of the other officers and ran into the barracks to find the perpetrator. It wasn't long before they picked Bruno out of the group and dragged him in to stand before me and report the incident. I told the accusing officer that he needed to put it the complaint in writing and note if he suspected anyone. He said he had already penned a written statement and he accused Bruno of the crime. He handed me the statement. I looked at Bruno and then dismissed the officers.

When the others had left and it was just the two of us, I approached Bruno and asked him to explain his side of the story. Bruno offered no defense and confessed to the act right away. He looked up at me and waited calmly for my reaction, as if he had been in trouble all his life and that this experience of waiting for his punishment was nothing new to him. "Don't worry about a thing." I said to him. I crumpled up the paper and tossed it into the trash can. I knew then that Bruno and I would become good friends.

I learned that Bruno was quite a character. He often told me outrageous stories of the things he did while he was in the NKVD jail. One time while he was held in the prison cell at Kharkiv, he desperately tried to find a way to be sent to a hospital as a means of escape. First, he wanted to come down with an illness. That didn't work. Then he wanted someone to break his leg, but could find no volunteers. One day he jumped out of a window in order to land on his leg and break it. Unfortunately the stunt didn't work as he didn't manage to break any bones, but he did make his leg really sore. He was a real daredevil and tried all kinds of crazy things. He told me so much about himself and his views of the world. I enjoyed his company and listened to his stories, but I offered very little information about me in return. I was always very careful not to let him find out who I really was. I did not trust anyone here.

A few days after I first met Bruno I noticed yet another new face in the camp that caught my attention. He was a lieutenant from the eleventh company and it was clear he was given the assignment of observing me. After the morning report this man approached me and asked if I were a Pole. I told him yes. He went on to ask me if I spoke German, and I replied that I could only speak a little German. I've heard this one before. You would think that the NKVD would try a new tactic. He boasted that he could speak very good German and that he was a Jew. He proceeded to have a conversation with me in German, but I answered him always in broken sentences. I knew right away what was going on and how to play this game.

The next morning I was visited by a Major from the NKVD and he offered me an assignment. He knew that I had been speaking with this man from the eleventh company. He asked me to find out if he was a Jew, where he last worked, and where he last resided. The Major told me that he had heard that the Lieutenant speaks very good German and may be able to serve as a translator. He also warned me that the man was armed and had a history of mistreating Russian prisoners. The NKVD found it was difficult to get anything out of this guy, but I may be one person in the camp who could get close to him. I told the Major I would carry out his order.

The Lieutenant from the eleventh company followed me around all the next day. I made it a point to always speak to him in broken German. I took notes of our conversations. The following day I reported back to the NKVD. In my report I said that he was a Jew and that the S.S. murdered his parents and his sister. He worked for the Germans in a labor camp in Kiev as a translator. As I made my report to the NKVD major, he seemed ambivalent about my accomplishments. He told me I had done good work and then instructed me to no longer keep an observation on him.

The act was all too familiar. The next day the man had suddenly disappeared from the camp and was not seen again. I told captain Tarrakanov all about what happened. He said: "Oskar, I told you right from the start you need to be careful. That man also asked me a few questions about you. He told me that he was a Jew so I spoke a bit of Hebrew to him but he could hardly answer me. I knew he was not a Jew, just another NKVD officer."

It had been nearly four months since I arrived in the camp. The days were becoming routine. During my evening walks with Anitschenko and Scharappil I would often fall silent to leave the two of them engaged in conversation. I was happy to make their acquaintance and would like to have considered them as friends, but I knew that I could not let my guard down and be a true friend to them. They spoke often of their families, their desires, their views of the war, thoughts and feelings that allowed me to understand them. Many times in turn they asked me open-ended questions, but I would offer only short answers. Eventually they stopped trying and just accepted my silent company. I felt like I had disappointed them, but then again these were my captors. I didn't owe them anything.

Was I really safer this way? Perhaps I should have remained on the other side as a prisoner. I needed only to survive and obey the rules. I was reasonably confident that eventually the war would end and we would all be released, at least those of us who were still alive. But I chose comfort instead, and that came with a price. If anyone here discovered that I was a German soldier I would be executed. That revelation could come from anyone, an NKVD spy or one of the officers or even one of my friends. One mistake was all it would take.

Chapter 12 ORDER AND DISCIPLINE

Death was commonplace in the camp. It came from those who did not survive the quarantine, those who fell ill from malnutrition or disease, and from those who did not obey the rules. Every day someone somewhere would report a dead body in the barracks or on the camp grounds, and with death came the duty of disposing of the corpses. That was a job for the prisoners. It was grueling work for men already so weak from malnutrition, illness, and physical abuse. The ground was still frozen hard in most places. The shovels and picks were icy cold and painful to handle as they struck the surface to loosen the rock and soil. So much labor was required from men having so little strength left, men who were all too aware of how close they were to landing in one of those holes themselves.

The graves were situated on the outskirts of the camp. The prisoners who dug them were under very close observation, but even with the added security two men managed to escape one day. Both were married. One had four children and the other had two. Guards were dispatched to retrieve them. Four days later they were recaptured and brought back to the camp. A public trial was held for them on March eighth, about a month before I met Bruno, with all of the prisoners in the camp on hand to witness the event. In Russia, it is the custom for the people to participate in matters that come before a court. High-ranking officers of the NKVD served as the judges. They were seated on the balcony of the main administration building, the only two-story structure in the camp. The balcony overlooked a large open area in the camp, almost like a town square where large groups may assemble for occasions such as this. Although there were thousands of people huddled together in the square, it was oddly silent.

The officers emerged from the second story of the administration building and took their seats on the balcony. The camp commander summoned the first defendant and he was led by a guard to the judgment seat. The commander ordered the defendant to plead his case.

The prisoner stood up and in a voice that could be clearly heard by all he offered an explanation for his actions. He told the group that in 1941 he was with the Russian army and during the Battle of Kiev was captured by the Germans. The Germans released him and he made his way back to his home town. There he registered with the German authorities as a translator because he could understand a bit of German. "I took the job in order to sustain my family." He pleaded. "I did not shame my people." Judgment came quickly and he was sentenced to three years in Siberia, first because he was deemed a spy working for the Germans, and second because he had escaped. The judge stood up and read the verdict. Then he asked everyone if they agreed with the decision. Everyone answered in hushed voices that they understood.

Then it was time for the second offender to offer his defense. He explained that he was twenty-six years old, and married with two children. He told the judges his story.

"Until 1933 my parents owned a thirty-acre farm. The communists approached the house one day and announced they were seizing our property in the name of the

State. They took the horses and the cows and all of our equipment. When my father resisted he was banished to Siberia for ten years. At the time, I was fifteen years old. There were six children in our family. We were fatherless and evicted from our home. They relocated us to a village thirty kilometers away where we were forced to work in a labor camp. We had no possessions, other than the clothes that we were wearing. We all lived together in a small room in the camp."

"In 1940 I joined the red army and one year later war broke out with Germany. I disserted the army and went freely over to the German side. Anyone in my place would have done the same thing! The Russian army treated us very poorly, and we were all getting banished to Siberia for the slightest transgressions. I no longer wished to fight and defend the communist party. Shortly after the German army took me into custody they allowed me to leave the prison. I immediately reported to the police department in town as I was instructed. As the Germans made their retreat, I was captured and sent to this camp. I escaped from this place because I do not belong here. I declare to all of you that I will not support Russia until my father is brought back to my family!"

The judge stood up and declared his sentence. In twenty-four hours this person would be hanged to death here in the camp. It was a way to demonstrate to all the prisoners how firm the punishments are. The judge went on to say that such people have no place in Russia. He asked the masses if they understood the verdict, and everyone say 'yes'. The gallows were erected the next day, and early in the morning at four o'clock he was hanged. Many people gathered at the gallows when they awoke to see what had happened. They were greeted by the image of the consequence of disobedience. The authorities left the body hanging there for twenty-four hours as a gruesome deterrent.

A great purge of prisoners had begun around this time. Between April first and April fifteenth, 1944 a total of seven thousand men were banished from the camp to prisons in Siberia. The sentences varied between three and twenty years. There were high-ranking Russian officers among them. An additional three thousand men were sent from the Camp to a penal colony on the front. These were people who worked for the Germans in the labor camp. Some of those were forced to work in mines under heavy guard.

The camp remained quite crowded despite the exodus of so many prisoners. Conditions were marginally better in the barracks with fewer mouths to feed and more room to sleep. I carried out my duties rather mechanically. I didn't complain and I didn't stand out.

I often wondered what fate had befallen my comrades from the German army. Where was the front now? There was very little news of the war trickling into camp. Most of what I had heard made it appear that the Russians had gained the upper hand and were forcing the German troops back away from Moscow. I didn't know how much of it too believe, as I'm sure the information coming in to us was filtered and perhaps outright fabricated to boost morale. One thing was for sure, the German forces did not reach this place.

The days were fairly routine. Most camp transgressions were minor incidents and not made into such a public spectacle as the hanging we witnessed a few weeks before. When there was trouble it usually involved petty theft or disorderly conduct, but even those could quickly turn into big problems. This was especially the case when they involved the theft of food. One such incident began when three platoons from our company were ordered to travel two kilometers to a nearby village baker to bring back bread for the camp. When they returned and inventoried the provisions they found that something was missing, and it was blamed on the platoon. After a brief investigation we suspected that two men from my platoon had taken six kilograms of bread, but we could not prove anything. As a result the entire company would be made to suffer, for when the bread was later distributed to the company the group received six kilograms less than what they otherwise would have been entitled to. That caused quite a ruckus. One lieutenant hollered "Why should I be responsible for this? These two stole the bread and for that I have my share taken away from me!" He reported the incident to Captain Tarrakanov, who promptly sent for the two men. They stubbornly denied everything, and in disgust he eventually dismissed them. The Captain didn't care either way. To him there was no harm done and it was just the same. Everything seemed settled as the men eventually calmed down, or so we thought.

Later that evening I was sitting together with Captain Tarrakanov and Lieutenant Scharappil. Shortly after nine o'clock we heard a terrible scream coming from a room that was down the corridor. I sprang to my feet and ran toward the commotion with Tarrakanov following close behind me. The door to the third platoon was open, and I assumed the scream came from there. As I approach the room one of the prisoners slumped into my arms, covered in blood. Tarrakanov and I took the man into our room. We saw that it was the same lieutenant that made the report accusing the two men of stealing the bread. He was attacked while he slept, beaten with his boots so badly that his face was a bloody mess. Tarrakanov was annoyed because he was now obligated to report this to the camp authorities. The NKVD quickly dispatched three soldiers to our barracks and all three men were taken away, the beaten lieutenant and the two accused. The punishment from the camp management was swift and quite severe. For the next twenty-five days, the men were deprived of two hundred grams of bread and a half liter of soup.

So much of my time each day in the camp was spent suppressing negative feelings. After all, I was a prisoner here myself, only my incarceration was more comfortable than the poor wretches that I was made to guard. I tried very hard to project an atmosphere of being aloof and ambivalent. I didn't want people to approach me, and let that show in my mannerisms. I didn't look at people directly. I didn't seek company. I didn't smile. It became second nature, and I worried that I may be permanently scarring my personality with this effort. I also worked hard to shut out the pain I felt from the death and despair that filled the camp environment. I assumed that over time I would become hardened by the misery and hardly notice it. I did not reach that point, at least not yet, and it had begun to wear on me.

I did find moments when I could indulge myself in a pleasant or comical distraction and afford a secret laugh. I remember one day around this time when one of our platoons was ordered to report for labor. I was with Tarrakanov in his quarters. The platoon leader entered the room and interrupted our conversation.

"Sir, there is a first lieutenant who refuses to come to work."

Tarrakanov put his hand up to his face to rub his eyes. He put his hand back down and gave the platoon leader a look as though he were asked to referee a dispute between two four-year-olds. "Alright, send him in."

The platoon leader disappeared and a minute later the first officer entered the room. Tarrakanov spoke to the officer in a most condescending tone. "Why are you not willing to report for work today?"

"I *am* willing to work, sir," the officer replied, "but I do not have any gloves."

"And where are your gloves, Lieutenant?"

The officer answered quite matter-of-factly "I am using my gloves to store some bread that I have saved. I don't want the others to know that I have it."

With that, Tarrakanov let out a boisterous laugh. I had never seen him laugh so hard. Even the officer couldn't hide his amusement at the site of his imposing commander enjoying this moment of comedy. When he could catch his breath he labored to tell the officer "Get out of here!"

Tarrakanov turned to me and chuckled a bit more. "You can see how clever the officers are in Russia?" Even I had had to laugh.

Later that evening there was another food incident. For the final meal of the day, each company received its portion of soup in a large vat. Lieutenant Anitschenko was responsible for distributing rations and divided the bread and soup. The kitchen was often generous when giving out the soup and there were usually fifteen to twenty liters more than what was otherwise rationed. The company was three hundred men strong and everyone wanted a share of that extra soup. As the vat made its round during the soup distribution, a great hoard of men followed it around closely in order to get an extra share. As they all crowded around the vat, some pushing and shoving ensued until eventually someone bumped into the vat. It tipped over and spilled all of its contents. The men were upset and fell silent at the wasted food. As for me, I just had to laugh. I thought to myself that this would have never happened in Germany because order and discipline would rule in this camp.

By far, the most bizarre incident occurred just a few days later. This time the joke was on me, and it nearly cost me my life. We were coming upon the First of May which is a special holiday in Russia. The entire camp was busy making preparations for a day of festivities including a demonstration parade for the camp leadership. Several companies were required to take part in this presentation including my own. The day would begin with sporting events and other games. Immediately following the games a Colonel from the NKVD out of Moscow would arrive to lead a formal march. He arrived early to take part in the practices that we held in the days leading up to the holiday event. It was clear that the officers in camp were taking this very seriously, probably in an effort to impress the top brass in Moscow.

The colonel started the parade. A mass of people followed behind. Among them was a man dressed in a German uniform. He made himself out to look like Adolf Hitler. He had a rocking horse between his legs and was pretending to flee the Russian lands. Following close behind Hitler was the German army. They were portrayed by a group of men dressed in German uniforms. Some had genuine German army shirts, others had the boots, and they all had their ears covered. When I saw the group assembled, I wondered about the fate of the men from whom the uniforms were taken. They could have been worn by my comrades from my battalion. I could not think long on it though, for risk of standing out as someone who didn't belong. All around me the men were having fun, enjoying a welcome diversion from the dreariness of this prison. Spring had arrived and the weather was turning warmer. The news of the war that reached the camp gave hope to the Russian army that they were indeed beating back the German forces. The mood was much happier, but not for me.

The men laughed out loud at the stunts and jokes they prepared. Some of the phony German soldiers used stilts, they pretended to make their escape out of the camp. They zigzagged to the left and to the right waving their arms comically as they pretended to follow Hitler on his horse on his way out of Russia.

The parade then continued with another group of men following behind the goofy Germans. They were pretending to be the Russian people chasing the German army away. The men waved their fists and shouted at the Germans in front of them as everyone made their way past the viewing stand. After this spectacle, our company followed behind marching in formal parade formation. I was selected to lead the company in this march. We took the whole thing very seriously, as the company started preparing for this event a full fourteen days in advance. Tarrakanov was determined to put on a grand display for his superiors.

May First had arrived and it was time to start the festivities. Everything proceeded as we had planned and it appeared that the camp leaders in the viewing stand were enjoying the show. Everyone laughed at the German Army. They hooted and hollered with the Russian people chasing them away. Finally it came time for our company to march.

Captain Tarrakanov reminded me several times over the past two weeks that it was my duty to put on a good display. We were all lined up on formation, and I admit I was quite nervous. I worked so hard over the past few months to remain unnoticed. In a few moments I would be a spectacle, the center of attention for the entire camp and the NKVD officers. It was the last thing I wanted here. But I owed a great deal to Tarrakanov. This performance was important to him and he was counting on me.

Tarrakanov turned to the group and yelled "Attention!" Then he shouted out "Okay, Oskar, show us what you can do!"

What happened next remained a mystery to me for many years. I suppose in some way a part of me blacked out, lapsing in to some sort of sub-consciousness while my instincts took over from years of training. I started my march, performing my best "belt-high" step for the Captain. After a few paces I realized what I was doing, and almost stopped dead in my tracks. My, God, what have I done? Have I just exposed my German identity by goose-stepping right in front of a collection of Russian military officers? The whole camp was watching me. What should I do? Then it got even worse. I turned around and saw that my entire company took my lead, and they were all goose-stepping behind me. I couldn't stop now, it had to look intentional. So I continued, and behind me the entire company proceeded to goose-step right past the viewing stand where the NKVD leaders were watching in amusement.

I tried not to look at the officers as we made our way past the stands. All I wanted was to get to the end and go hide somewhere. The march was only a few minutes long, but it seemed to last for hours. People were laughing, pointing at me, and saying things to each other. I was convinced that I just secured a place in front of the firing squad. My heart raced and I was sweating, but I could not let anyone notice that this wasn't intentional. And what will Tarrakanov think?

To my utter disbelief this turned out to be no disaster. Instead, Tarrakanov was quite proud of my march. When the parade route came to an end I stopped and stood still while the men around me broke formation. They laughed and chided each other. Many of them approached me, patted me on the back and thanked me for putting on such a good performance. I smiled to everyone, but I was still in shock.

I looked for Tarrakanov and saw him approach the viewing stand to speak with the colonel. He later told me that the NKVD officers called him over to ask about the man who had that great march. Tarrakanov replied that it was a Polish first lieutenant. It was clear that the colonel enjoyed this march. After a brief exchange, Tarrakanov jogged over to our spot and ordered the men who took part in the march to gather around. He pointed at me and gestured to come over to him. I made my way through the assembly, and when I reached the captain he put his hand on my shoulder.

"I just spoke with the colonel. He enjoyed your march so much that he wants to see it again. Gather the men back at the starting point."

I just stared back at him. I couldn't think of anything to say.

"Go!" he shouted and turned to walk back to the viewing stand.

I rounded up the men and together we walked quickly back at the start where we fell into formation for another go. From a distance, I could see Tarrakanov schmoozing with the officers in the stands. I kept him in my sight waiting for his signal to start. When he waved to me, I took a deep breath and started my belt-high march again. I heard the stomping of feet behind me and the sound of laughter, but I dared not look around this time. The officers applauded as we marched by and I gave a polite nod to Tarrakanov. He was clearly quite proud of me. I, however, was still in disbelief over what had just taken place.

We completed our second march past the viewing stand and the crowd broke up more quickly this time. I tried to melt away out of sight with the group, but one of the colonels called out my name. I looked over and he waved me over to speak with me. I jogged over to his spot and saluted.

"What is your name, soldier?"

"Oskar Scheja."

"Well, Oskar Scheja, you put on quite a performance today."

"Thank you, sir." I answered bluntly.

"Your commander tells me that you have made a request to rejoin the Polish army. Is that true?"

Still standing at attention I replied, "That is correct."

"Well, I would like you instead to consider joining the Russian army. It would be far better than serving in the Polish army. We have much more to offer you."

I could hardly believe this was really happening.

"It is all the same to me, whether I am with the Russian or the Polish army."

With that his demeanor quickly changed, and he decided he would waste no more time with me. He waved his hand at me and said, "Very well." Then he turned to join the other NKVD officers. I assume that I had been dismissed. I turned and put as much distance between me and the NKVD officers as I could.

I learned from Captain Tarrakanov later that afternoon that the colonel called the Captain over to him a second time in an effort to convince me again to enter the Russian army. When the Captain came back he suggested that I make another visit over to the colonel. Tarrakanov made the arrangements for me, but I declined. That was an encounter I would have no part of. I wanted to put this incident as far behind me as possible.

Chapter 13 CAMP 280

There was a new arrival in the ninth company later
that month. His name was Josef Malinowski, a Polish
officer who supposedly came from Lemberg. Captain
Tarrakanov seemed eager to introduce us to each other,
apparently taking the role of social director for connecting
all of the Polish citizens in camp. I had a conversation with
Malinowski and he shared with me that at one time he had
been a chief medical officer with the German army. He was
captured and taken prisoner by the Russians in Odessa.
While in custody there the Russians put his skills to use,
employing him to treat civilians in the city wounded by the
fighting. All the while he insisted that he was in fact an
officer in the Polish army. The Russians eventually
concluded they had no more use for him, or that he was too
much of a risk for escaping so they assigned him to this
NKVD camp.

Now there were three Polish officers here including
Bruno. Over time we learned that we were the only Poles
out of the fifteen thousand people that were in the camp.
Everyone else was Russian. I was surrounded by my
enemies, assuming an identify that shielded me from
execution. How long that shield would serve me, I did not
know. The urge to leave this place began to swell inside me.
It had been many weeks since I made my formal appeal to
re-join the Polish army. I felt it was time to try again. I

gathered Bruno and the doctor one evening in a quiet part of the camp and told them that we need to find a way out of here. Collectively we approached one of the camp commanders and submitted a formal request to be transferred out of this camp and serve with the Polish army. The commander took the request with a distinct air of indifference and instructed us to wait for the response.

One week later we did hear a response, but it was not what we had hoped for. I was summoned by an NKVD major who told me that a combined request is not permitted. We needed to resubmit each one individually, in writing. Then he let me leave. I informed Bruno and the Doctor and we did just that. Then we waited some more.

Four days later, something unusual happened. The Doctor had disappeared. I learned that he was transported along with about two thousand other men to "Etapp". "Etapp" meant forced labor in a cabbage field about eighty kilometers east of Stalino. That was the last time I ever saw him. Now there were just two Poles in the camp. A few days had past and I assumed that this request, like the last one, would go nowhere.

I was wrong. One afternoon Tarrakanov found me on the grounds and instructed me to visit one of the NKVD officers in the camp. He told me to bring Bruno with me. I had an uneasy feeling about this. Surely it was in reference to our request, but it could also mean bad news for the two of us. One never could tell when the NKVD was involved. We approached the officer together, nervously standing at attention while we waited to hear the reason for this meeting. I was relieved to learn that our transfer request was granted. I buried that feeling deep inside, so as not to reveal that this meant one step closer to freedom and not simply a desire to continue the fight.

Our assignment wasn't exactly what I would have preferred, but it was a step in the right direction. We were instructed to report to a prisoner of war camp where German soldiers were held. This camp was located eighteen kilometers east of Stalino, known as camp 280 division 1. We set out on foot from camp 240 at eleven o'clock in the morning with one officer and four other men. When the gate swung open for us I let slip a big grin. I knew that I wasn't yet free but for a moment it sure felt that way. It was a beautiful day, perfect for spending it outside. For the first time I carefully examined the landscape around me, and Russia no longer looked like such a dreary place. Bruno and I smiled to each other from time to time, but never said a word. It was quite dark by the time we arrived, around ten o'clock that evening. I was looking forward to seeing German soldiers again and to be with my own people. The camp administration met us at the gate and brought us inside. The officer from the previous camp who accompanied us handed to the guard instructions that the two Polish officers were to take over.

When we arrived at the administration building the camp management greeted us warmly. They led us straight to the doctor for a checkup. The doctor told us both to undress. He didn't examine us very closely as he saw right away that we kept our strength up. When the medic completed his paperwork, he handed it to us and the guard brought to the camp commander. The commander escorted us to a barrack where there was another guard waiting for us. The guard saluted to the commander and left.

That was when I heard the German language spoken again in its native tongue for the first time in what seemed like a very long time. The conversations came from the room next door. It brought a tear to my eyes. For a moment, I felt like I was home. The commander escorted us into a small room with two bedposts. He gave us two blankets and told us that in the morning we will review our duties and other matters. After the long march to Camp 280, we were very tired and happy to lie down.

Early the next morning at eight o'clock, we were visited by a Russian officer. He took us right into the mess hall. He announced to the kitchen staff that we were two Polish officers and entitled to receive officer's rations. This meant three hundred grams of white bread, three hundred grams of dark bread, twenty-five grams of sugar, and thirty grams of butter. We went with the officer to the same place where the prisoners ate and sat among them. There I met a German lieutenant and a German corporal who was a camp leader. The first commander was Lieutenant Böhner and the second was Corporal Taps from Nuremberg. The lieutenant took us around to meet the other German, Romanian, and Hungarian officers.

In all there were eighteen Germans, six Rumanians, and eleven Hungarian officers. Then they told us there were two Polish brigades stationed here and we met many of them as well. The Polish men were all happy to greet us as the news spread through the camp that two Polish officers had arrived. We were told that Poland had been liberated and the Polish army joined with the Russian army to fight against the Germans.

With that, I began to feel that coming here wasn't such a good idea. In fact, it may have made my situation even more untenable. I had been able to fool the Russians into believing that I was a Pole and not a German combatant but it may be even more difficult to deceive Germans and Poles. I understood the must be even more careful here so that no one finds out that I'm really a German. I was also afraid that I would run into someone that I knew personally. That would certainly end my entire charade. I had to continue this deception for a while longer.

On the second day, a stately man in a Russian uniform visited me. It was late in the afternoon and Bruno and I were lying on our bunks taking a break from the day's activities. When he came into our room I sprang to my feet, saluted, and in Russian stated clearly, "Stationed here are two Polish officers." But this man spoke in German to me. He asked me if I also spoke German, and I told him yes. He instructed me to join him in his barracks, number five, and asked me where he could find the instructor. I told him to follow me.

I took him to the administration building where we met the camp instructor. In a commanding voice that begged you to obey, he asked us both to accompany him to his quarters. Without question we followed him into building where he was staying. The meeting was uneventful as he asked fairly simple questions about the size and makeup of the prisoner population and the command structure. As soon as I had left his company, I sought out Lieutenant Böhner and asked him who this man was. He told me that he was a German communist who fled to Russian in 1933 when the Nazis came to power. He came from the Saarland area. He is employed by the Russians to give anti-fascism speeches to the prisoners of war.

A short time later, I received notice to report to the instructor and promptly complied. I had a very odd exchange with the man, making me feel a bit uneasy about my situation here. I stood in the doorway of his office and waited for him to focus his attention on me. The instructor was seated at a desk concentrating on a document he was writing. When he looked up, he asked me to take a seat in front of his desk. As I took my seat, he readied himself by clearing off an area of his desk and took out a new notepad.

The instructor asked me for my first and last names which he recorded dutifully. Then he asked me for my rank and about the responsibilities I had in the Polish army. After I answered, he remarked that I can speak very good German. Since I've been here among so many Germans, I didn't try to hide that so much. I told him that I learned German in school. He asked me if I also spoke English and French and I told him that I could. I was comfortable telling him all this because he had shared with me that he was formerly just a locksmith's assistant. There was no way that he could speak English or French, so he was not in a position to challenge me on that. He next asked me if I would answer some questions about politics. I told him: "I never have been interested in politics and never will be. One thing that's clear to me is that a soldier could never become a politician, nor can a politician become a soldier."

He looked up at me with a blank face, then down at his notepad to precisely record my reply. His last question was if I were a brother of Hitler. I answered him "I bet you recognize everyone right on the nose." He wrote some more in his notepad, then thanked me for my visit and told me to send my comrade in.

I walked back to my barracks to find Bruno and told him to visit the instructor. He asked me what it was about but I couldn't really say. Bruno left then returned about twenty minutes later. He told me about his conversation, which appeared to be a bit livelier than the one that I had with the instructor. I thought this camp was going to be different, but it's shaping up to be more of the same. Fortunately, we both come into this camp with an understanding of how the NKVD works. It may start with the instructor, but it ends with the NKVD.

The next morning a first lieutenant from the NKVD came into our quarters. The conversation started out rather pleasantly, asking us how we were acclimating and if we liked our new surroundings. His Polish wasn't very good so he asked Bruno and me if we understood Russian. When we answered that we did, he was a bit relieved. He turned to me and asked me to which outfit I belonged in the Polish military. I evaded the question, telling him only that I was with lieutenant and Bruno ensign. He asked us if we were ever officers in the German army. We told him no, that we were both only in a German construction crew for a short time. He continued talking with us about our experiences in the army, but kept coming back to the question of whether we were German officers. Eventually he gave up, said good-bye and left the room rather abruptly.

That last conversation gave me a very uncomfortable feeling. I told Bruno we need to be careful here. We need to ask around if there are other people here from the area we came from who may know us. He agreed, and the two of us set out around the camp to mill about the prisoner population to learn more about where they came from.

That evening Bruno brought me the news. He said "Oskar, there is someone else here from my home town. I haven't spoken with him yet. He works in the store room. Let's go there together right now."

We looked around and found the man. He was a Pole from Grudziadz in the Danzig region. I asked him which street he lived on and by coincidence it turned out he lived on the same street as Bruno. We had some doubt about his answer, so we pressed him again. I asked him if perhaps he lived on the same street as someone named Schmagelski. He said there was someone by that name, but that he had been living in Germany for many years. Bruno believed now that he was speaking about his cousin. He said his cousin was also from that area, but lived on a different street. That may have been the only thing that saved Bruno.

Next we concentrated on trying to find someone who may have come from my area. For the next few days I meandered around the camp casually asking different people where they were from. I was lucky, for the entire time I spent in the camp I never once met anyone who knew me. I also made sure also to stay away from the camp administration area.

This prison camp was very similar to Camp 240. Both were hastily erected in the middle of a vast, open area that was once farmland. The crudely constructed buildings were outlined with a deep tangle of barbed wire. Things did appear to be more structured and orderly in this camp. That was surely due to the presence of so many Germans, who were much more disciplined than their Russian counterparts. Wake up call was early at five o'clock, and at five thirty we stepped outside for inspection and counting. Breakfast was served punctually at six o'clock. They gave each of us a liter of soup. It was very thin and had coarse grains of corn. We were supposed to have been served two hundred grams of bread, which after being weighed on a Russian scale come out as only about eighty grams. If the work brigade met their quota for the day they received an additional two hundred grams of bread. In the afternoon we received two hundred grams of bread, another liter of soup, and fifty grams of Grouper. The fish was cooked, sliced thick and seasoned with sunflower oil. At dinner time, we received two hundred grams of bread, a small cup of coffee, and one hundred grams of a different fish that was a bit smaller.

At twelve o'clock in the afternoon the work detail took a break. Those who did not go to work stayed inside and received some medical attention. The work brigade returned at six o'clock in the evening after a long day that began early in the morning at seven o'clock. At six thirty, it was time for the evening prisoner count, and after that it was time to eat. Curfew was at ten o'clock in the evening. Every barrack was assigned a waking guard. If anyone had to get up in the night the guard was responsible for making sure that person returned.

Once a month, every prisoner was examined by a doctor to make every man was maintaining his strength. Prisoners were graded according to their strength and health. Those in category one were cleared to work in the factory loading heavy, one hundred kilogram bombs that were being transported to the Front. Each man is expected to load one hundred and seven pieces in eight hours. Each bomb needed to be carried between fifty and one hundred and twenty meters. Category two people were those who were dropped from category one because they were not as strong. They also worked in the factory carrying fifty kilogram grenades.

They needed to load one hundred and fifty grenades in eight hours. If the labor brigade achieved their goal they received the extra ration of bread.

The category three people were not as strong. They did cleanup in the factory, stocked shelves, and kept things in order. Then there was a group that was for those who were being rehabilitated, which was category four. They were assigned only for light clean up duty around the camp. Lastly, there was a group we called the "schlapp-commandos". They were so broken down and undernourished that all of those who tried to go into a higher category fell back into the broken commandos within three weeks because the work was so hard and they had received such poor care.

The conditions were difficult for the laborers. They spent the night on bare, wooden planks. During the winter, the barracks were heated by an oven for which we were allowed one lump of coal. The laborers were not given any blankets, only a coat that at night served as your blanket. If you felt sick and could not to work but did not receive a medic's approval for being excused, you received three days of prison time. Those were the harsh regulations of the administration of camp 280, first division.

One afternoon I was speaking with Lieutenant Böhner. We were enjoying a pleasant conversation when after a while he told me that if I were a Polish officer, then I must have also served in the German army at one time. I replied casually that I was never in the Polish army. He gave me a stern look, abruptly ended our conversation, and turned to immediately report the matter. I knew I was in a bit of trouble. I returned to my bunk to concoct a story that I hoped would be good enough to allow me to wiggle out of this.

That night around two o'clock I was awoken from my sleep by a guard who demanded that I immediately report to camp administration building. When I entered the building, an NKVD officer was waiting for me. He escorted me into his office and pointed to a short desk which had a pencil and a sheet of paper on it. I sat in a small chair at the desk and waited for instructions. The paper contained a questionnaire with general questions about my background. The officer instructed me to complete it. I peppered the form with more false statements, hoping that I was cunning enough continue to play out my deception. I wrote that I attended the Gymnasium, was admitted to the Polish officer's academy, and became an ensign. In 1930, I traveled to France to the Elsass-Lothringen region and then on to Metz. I attended a local agricultural school and in 1933 I became an agricultural inspector.

A woman, clearly also from the NKVD, joined the lieutenant to keep an eye on me and oversee the matter. I stayed in that office filling out forms until four o'clock before I was excused. I returned to my bunk exhausted, drained by the experience. I was becoming more nervous about my situation here. As I lay there, I tried hard to remember precisely what I had written, for I knew that I would need to recall it in order to keep my stories straight. The morning wakeup call seemed to come only a minute or two after I finally fell asleep again.

Two days later there was another visit in the middle of the night from the NKVD, and I was instructed to answer the same questions as before. Then there came a third such visit. This exercise was repeated a few times over the course of the next several days, during which time they made me complete eight questionnaires. All of them were the same. Bruno was also experiencing the same harassment. Something was definitely wrong.

Ten days later Bruno and I were called in front of the officer's board in the command barracks. We took our positions and stood nervously before the men in uniform assembled in front of us. There were three camp commanders seated behind a long table. After affirming our identity, one of the men came right to the point and announced to us that if we had indeed also served officers in the German army that we would our lose standing in the camp command structure. We did not respond. The officers reviewed our questionnaires and pressed us on the validity of our answers but we stood by our statements. My heart grew heavy as it was clear where this was headed. In the end it was no use. The NKVD officers in this camp weren't buying our story. My fortune had turned again. I was stripped of my position as a camp officer and assigned to the labor force. The same fate fell to Bruno. Before we knew what had happened, we were assigned to work in the factory loading bombs with the rest of the prisoners.

After the officers announced their decision they quickly left the room. Two guards that had stood next to us during the hearing escorted us back to our quarters. Our belongings were confiscated, including the uniforms we were wearing. I was given a filthy set of clothes; a shirt, pants, socks, and boots. I was sure that the man who last wore these clothes was lying in a hole in the ground, somewhere at the edge of the camp. I didn't say a word. I thought I would be filled with sadness after losing so much, but that wasn't it. It was more like resolution. I had escaped death before, not only by my enemy's hand, but also by my own. I had beaten the Russian in a game of deception. I survived this long. I knew I could beat them again.

There was no time for further contemplation. It was still morning and we were quickly rushed over to the factory to join the work force. Though I was in reasonably good condition, I was not accustomed to the hard labor I was quickly subjected to. The bombs were heavy to lift and there seemed to be an endless supply of them. By the time the shift was over, I was exhausted. Though the wooden planks that I slept on were hard and unforgiving, it mattered not to me as I fell asleep right away.

The next two days came and went very quickly. The daylight hours were filled with the repetitive motion of lifting and loading. My muscles ached. It became hard to focus on anything other than getting past the next bomb to lift. Still I held on to hope that someday I would be able to get out of here. From time to time I would take a moment to gaze around the factory floor. There were several guards on duty watching over us but they were often drunk. The same was true of the guards at the barracks. That offered an opportunity and some hope.

Chapter 14 THE STREETS OF KIEV

Three days after I was stripped of my ranking and reassigned to the prisoner population, there was a big commotion in the camp. Rumors were spreading quickly that we were to be relocated. That afternoon the factory was emptied and every able-bodied prisoner was summoned to a large open area. The guards divided us into five groups and each formed a line in front of a table. One by one every prisoner was handed a pair of leather shoes that resembled army boots. They also gave us an additional pair of wooden shoes. We all wondered what was going on. We collected our new footwear and proceeded to another station where a doctor was waiting for us. The medic gave each of us an examination. Those that passed were handed one of a number of different cooking items such a ladle or a small pot. When I was finished I was in possession of a very odd collection of wares. We were told to sit on the ground and wait for further instructions.

At two o'clock that afternoon, a number of guards approached the collection of people waiting patiently on the dusty camp ground, and searched the pockets of each prisoner who was certified by the doctors as being healthy enough for whatever came next. There were seventeen hundred men who had made it through the exam. We remained seated there for the rest of the afternoon. The

Russians even went so far as to serve us our evening rations in our place.

Shortly after the meal, we learned why the camp administrators went to such lengths to make sure we were healthy. At seven o'clock in the evening the guards orders us to stand up. They marched us out from the camp in a long column. A watchman was stationed every ten meters along our route. Once we hit the road, they made us run at such a pace that was hardly possible to keep up. We covered four kilometers in twenty minutes. We ended our run at a small train station. It was dark and I could not tell if it was the same station that I came to when I arrived at camp 240. There were many cattle cars standing by on the tracks in front of the station and we were loaded into them. The prisoners were grouped by nationality. We had separate cars for Germans, Poles, French, Romanians, Hungarians, and Finns. When the last prisoner was stuffed into the wagons, the doors were locked and the windows strung with barbed wire. They kept us in there for a good hour before the train started to move. There were so many packed in each car that there was no room to sit, so we all stood shoulder to shoulder.

It was night time and the sky was cloudy, so we couldn't tell what direction we were moving in. Before we boarded we noticed that guards had brought food and a means of preparing meals with them into one of the cars, so we concluded that we were in for a long journey. As the train made its way across the countryside, we were jostled around so much by the shaking that we frequently fell over on to each other. Our legs ached and the air was foul. The constant banging of bodies against one another made for frayed nerves. I thought to myself that in Germany the cows traveled more comfortably than the people do in Russia.

When daylight came, we were able to determine that our direction was northwest. The wagons warmed up very quickly with the heat of the sun bearing down on it from outside and the mass of bodies packed together on the inside. By noon, the temperature in the carriages was nearly unbearable. I labored for every breath. As we passed by the railroad station of the towns along the way, the train would slow down to a crawl. There were villagers lined up along the tracks. The people spat on us, waived their fists, and threw stones as we rode by. They chanted "death to the Fritzes" and shouted obscenities.

We made two stops that day, each for a meal which consisted of a liter of soup, six hundred grams of dry bread, and a half liter of water. More important than the food and drink was the opportunity to be out in the fresh air. The guards dragged us off the car, leading us out of the way to make sure there was room for the rest of the passengers to be offloaded. We collapsed to the ground as soon as we were free of the guard and gasped for breath. Our reprieve only lasted long enough to distribute the food. In a few minutes time the guards pulled us up off the ground and threw us back into the wagon. We repeated this process the following day and night. On the third day, the train stopped for the last time and we finally arrived at our destination. The Russians unloaded us, but gave us no time to rest. There were troop transport vehicles waiting at the railway stop. The guards quickly loaded us into the trucks and drove us into a large square. None of the prisoners spoke and no one gave us any hint of what they had in store for us. As we drove through the streets it was clear that we were in a large city, one that had been the target of German artillery. I recognized this place. It was the city of Kiev. Three years ago I rejoiced at its capture. We spent five days here after winning the battle. How odd it was for me to return like this.

When we arrived at the main square, I was able to fully absorb the great spectacle that the Russians had planned. Thousands of people were lined up along the perimeter, dozens deep. They gawked at the great mass of ragged bodies assembled in the middle of the square before them. Tanks were stationed every two hundred meters in line with the crowd of civilians, their cannons pointed threateningly in our direction. Large machine gun towers were erected at each corner, and Russian soldiers were perched at the top of each one to keep a watchful eye on us. Within the square large, speakers were mounted on tall posts that blared out orders for us to follow in many languages. My transport came to a stop, allowing a small group of Russian soldiers to approach the vehicle and take charge of its contents. I paid no attention to the mechanical voices from the loudspeakers and simply followed the men in front of me. With machine guns pointed our way, we formed orderly lines inside the square.

It became clear to me what was happening. This was a propaganda event. The Russian authorities were using us to make a demonstration to the people of the prisoners they had taken and what they did with them. We were a trophy of the war and we all looked terrible. Since our selection for this trip, we were not permitted to shave. We were staged to appear as if we were recently captured from the front line. It was a show, a spectacle, and we were the main event. We waited patiently in the square in full view of the thousands of onlookers for the last truck to unload is prisoners and be ushered into place. I picked my head up to take in the entire view. There were a great many prisoners rounded up here; I would guess around twenty thousand. I could see bulky cameras stationed among the civilians pointed at us, as if the machine guns and tanks weren't enough to keep us in line.

After the final man was put in place, there was a signal that the event had begun. The crowd jeered at us. A loud voice crackled from the speakers providing cues for the city's inhabitants to respond with shouts, their fists held high. I paid no attention to any of it; I just wanted to crawl back into the train cars. I smiled to myself at the thought of choosing the train cars over the discomfort that I was feeling at the moment. I'm not sure if it was shame, or embarrassment, or even anger. I believe that above all, I felt thoroughly defeated. I was part of a team, we had a mission to accomplish, and we failed. All of us here in this square failed. I allowed my captors to have their time to gloat. They won this day, but for me it wasn't over. I wanted to crawl back into that cattle car, return to camp and survive! The game was still on, so long as I continued to draw breath.

After the speeches were over we began to move, but not onto transports. Instead we poured out onto the city streets. It was orderly and we were flanked by many Russian soldiers, who trained their weapons on us as if they dared any man to step out of line. We paraded through the city of Kiev, twenty thousand prisoners marching through the streets. On every corner there were cameras and reporters that filmed the event for the press. The government had declared a holiday for the civilians so that they may view the demonstration and be seen on camera packing the streets. I noticed that there were mostly women in the audience. With their fists held out they shouted things like, "Fritz, first we will rebuild Russia and then it's off to Siberia for you!" Several women threw stones at us. The column of prisoners meandered through the entire city, weaving through the streets for several hours until we arrived back at the railway yard. Then we were loaded like livestock back into the wagons, and the train to return us to our prison in the east. We were exhausted, but the density at which we were packed into the cars left us no room to lie down. Forced to stand again, we swayed back and forth as the train cut a path through the fields. The return trip took only two days and we came back to our camp near the city of Stalino.

Chapter 15 THE RETURN HOME

That night we returned I fell asleep quickly, being the first opportunity for me to lie down for a long stretch of time. Unfortunately, I would not be afforded much time to sleep. At three o'clock in the morning, an NKVD officer butted me in the chest with the end of his rifle to wake me. He ordered me to stand up and follow him. Barely awake, I walk outside with the officer following close behind, nudging me along until we arrived at one of the administration buildings. Before I knew it, I was seated in a chair in front of the desk of another NKVD officer who told me he had more questions for me. He asked me the same questions again and again. It was difficult for me to remember exactly how I answered them in the past, and after a while I stopped caring. At this point, I had no idea what they were trying to accomplish.

Daylight came. When the questioning had stopped I assumed that my work at the factory would continue, but there were more changes in store. My friend, Bruno, learned that he would not be joining me on the factory floor, but instead he was assigned to a Polish work brigade. Three days later they created a new brigade in the camp, penal brigade Fifty. That would become my assignment. The brigade was led by a Jew, Jude Brinkmann. There were people of all nations in this brigade, those who fled and those who got wise that their homeland was taken over by the SS or the Communist Party. This brigade was not permitted to work outside, but instead only within the camp buildings.

I discovered that the people of Russia regarded cleaning toilets as the lowest and worst form of punishment. That was the mission for the penal brigade, to clean the toilets from sun up to sun down. The guards assigned our brigade were even worse than the others in the camp. It was clear that this was a form of punishment for them as well. The guards seemed to always be drunk, which is probably why we weren't allowed anywhere near the perimeter of the camp. Their condition would make it easy for anyone to escape.

I didn't consider the work to be degrading as the Russians appeared to regard it. On the contrary, it was much easier than lugging around heavy bombs all day on the factory floor. Still, I wondered what these NKVD agents wanted to accomplish with me. During a break, I asked the Polish inspector why I was assigned to this position. He told me that they recently established this brigade and that I seemed to be the right man for the job. I was content to take that as a compliment. Perhaps this wasn't meant as punishment for me after all.

On my second day of work, I was happy to learn that my friend Bruno had also joined the unit. I could only imagine what he did to earn this assignment. A few days later, there were more changes as they moved Brinkman out and promoted me to his position as Brigadier. Clearly I was making an impression on someone. That created a lot of gossip in the camp. As usual, I kept to myself to allow everyone else to wonder and reach their own conclusions about me. This brigade was now forty-three men strong. It included two German chaplains and a German Lieutenant, Albrecht von Bieren. I learned that the Lieutenant had participated in the transport to Kiev with me.

A few days after I was promoted to Brigadier, I did some exploration to learn how much trust and influence I had earned with the leadership in camp. I asked for extra rations of bread for everyone in our brigade, because we were all cleared for factory work. They granted us two hundred grams more, but I had to promise that everyone must show that they're working hard. If they judged that not to be the case, I would receive ten years of banishment. I agreed, but later discovered that the extra two hundred grams of bread wasn't making us any stronger. It wasn't long before we were obliged to give up the extra rations.

The months past by and life in the camp became routine. It was the summer of 1944. The weather was warm. The work was unpleasant, but much less taxing on my body than the hard labor of the factory. The men in my brigade began to form relationships with the civilians that worked in the store rooms. I got to know a few of them as well. Over time, the prisoners learned to barter with the civilians. A prisoner, for example, may trade a pair of shoes for three kilograms of bread. Some even traded their pants and coats. I'm not ashamed to say that I also took part in the camp's black market. One time, I traded two hundred grams of bread for five cigarettes. I even traded pile of horse manure once for some bread.

It was around this time that I really began to despise the Romanians in camp. I never trusted them or held them in high regard, even when we were fighting on the same side. The Romanians in our camp appeared to have more freedom than the others. If, for example, a Romanian prisoner liked a

German soldier's shoes and wanted them, that evening in the barracks the Romanian would simply grab the shoes away from the German. If the German took the complaint to the commander it was the German who was locked up. The German soldiers were often beaten by the Romanians without provocation, even though they were at one time brothers in arms. I had heard stories that women and girls in Romania were often mistreated, beaten, raped, and burned. These violent acts by the Romanian men were now being carried out on German soldiers.

The Romanians would soon have more Germans to torment. One day, an additional two thousand prisoners arrived in our camp. They came from Bessarabia where the Romanians took German captives, and from what we were told they were held under the most deplorable conditions. The Romanian army had surrounded the Germans and told them to surrender with their weapons raised and nothing would happen to them. By that time the Germans had run out of ammunition and they had been without food for six days, so they came out with their weapons held high and surrendered. The Romanians quickly captured, robbed, and abused them. It was far worse than the way the Russians had treated the Germans. The Romanians also failed to provide any food for them. After keeping them for four additional days the Romanians eventually handed over the German prisoners to the Russian army. The Russians gave them food, loaded the prisoners into wagons, and brought them to our camp. Of the two thousand prisoners that were taken in by the Russians only half made it to Stalino alive. The rest perished during the ride over, mostly from typhoid.

A short time later on October eighth, an additional nine hundred and eighty-two men came to Stalino. They were also German prisoners held by the Romanian army, and they, too, were suffering from typhoid and immediately quarantined. Ten days later, eight hundred and thirty-six of them were dead.

There was another thing going on with the Romanians that made me resent them. In camp it was strictly forbidden to have contact with people who were sick and in quarantine. In spite of this rule, many Romanian prisoners would simply ignore it and hand water to their compatriots through the windows. They would also bring shoes, coats, rings, and more. They often removed clothing and other items from the dead and earned money selling it to civilians. Such was the life of the Romanians in camp, while the Germans were forced to load heavy bombs all day.

Lieutenant von Bieren and I became friends over time. He engaged in an interesting hobby in the camp. The Lieutenant was quite an artist and painted portraits of Russian officers. For that, he earned some extra bread and smokes. From time to time he would share those with me.

One day the two of us forged a plan to escape from the camp. As winter approached, they gave us new pullovers. We traded these to civilians for provisions we would need after we were out of the camp. On December twenty-fourth we planned to flee from our work detail, but two days before von Bieren fell got very sick and was reassigned to the schlapp commando team. I could not make it out of the camp without him and so our plan was shelved. It was a long recovery for von Bieren as he stayed with the schlapp-commando team for four months. I waited patiently for him to return to health.

We held on to our plan for escape, until one day my fortunes changed again. The camp leaders announced that all the Poles were to be released back to the Polish army. Every Polish citizen was ordered to report to the administration area for further instructions. Three different people came to bring me the news. The information they shared was encouraging, but no date was set for our release. Still it gave me hope that my time in Russian prison camps was soon to come to an end. I had been working with the night shift. That evening around twelve thirty I happened to be outside, when a streak of light suddenly appeared across the sky between the Little Dipper and the Big Dipper. It was brilliant and beautiful. It was there for about three minutes, disappeared, and reappeared. It did this four times. I stared up at the sky watching it intently. I was struck by this phenomenon and was sure it held some meaning.

Exactly one month later, Germany capitulated. Some part of me didn't want to believe the news, but deep down I expected it. For the past year I had heard from the Russian officers how the war had turned in their favor. I was sure that the information coming back to them was filtered to improve morale in the ranks, but the sight of battered German soldiers flowing into camp told a different story. Early at six o'clock in the morning on May ninth, the camp commander called together the entire prison population and made the announcement. All of the prisoners were elated to learn that they would finally be released and set free. A great cheer welled up from the gathering. The commander told us that the first group to be released was the Poles. I was wondering if that would include me, as the Poles were always talking among themselves about me, saying that I was no Pole but instead a German. Even the German officers began to doubt that I was really a Pole. As before, no date for our release was given, but the knowledge that it was coming lifted everyone's spirits, prisoners and guards alike.

Several weeks passed with no further announcement. Then on July first, 1945 the NKVD issued orders to release some of the Poles. News spread to every corner of the camp for the Poles to gather in front of the main administration building at noon. Shortly before that time, I found Bruno and we walked silently the rest of the way together. We were both happy, but had reason to be nervous. Promptly at twelve o'clock an NKVD officer emerged from the building to address the men assembled before him. After a brief introduction that I could not hear clearly, he started reading off the names of those who were the first to be released. I waited anxiously until I heard the sound of my name being called out. A feeling of relief rushed over me. I almost fainted. It was like a heavy stone was lifted off my heart. A short time later I heard Bruno's name. I turned to him and smiled. For a moment, he stood still facing the officer who had just given him the best news of his life. Then he became emotional and began to cry. He turned in my direction and smiled back, then threw his arms around me.

"We did it, Oskar. We've made it," he whispered quietly.

"Yes we did," was all I could say.

After the last names were read, the crowd began to disperse. A German colonel approached me and put his hand on my shoulder. "Oskar," he said. "Get off one station before Warsaw. Do not walk out a free man together with the rest of the Polish soldiers. Men like us are only found in the German army."

My heart skipped a beat as I quickly looked into his eyes. I must have had a look of shock on my face, but he offered only a smile in return and with that turned and walked away. I thought on it for a minute and concluded that I need not be concerned. I did not want anything to keep me from enjoying this moment. It was a time for quiet and inward celebration.

On July thirteenth, 1945 Bruno and I waited at the camp entrance along with a few dozen other Polish prisoners. The mood was light and the people gathered there joked with one another. The guards remained serious as they waited for the order to open the gate. When the command was given, the gate was pushed open and the men streamed through. Bruno and I stepped out of the camp together for the first time without guards watching us and weapons pointed in our direction. That was indeed the happiest day of my life.

We walked as a group along the dirt road to the railway yard in Stalino. We were a sorry-looking bunch, but we didn't care. No one carried any possessions as we had none. We must have been quite a sight when we entered the town and walked through the streets to the station. We collected many dirty looks and a fair number of obscenities were shouted in our direction, but we paid them no attention. We didn't even look back. There were Russian guards at the train station who were expecting our arrival. They instructed us to wait one more day before we could board a train that would bring us to Warsaw. We spent the night on the ground outside of the building. The night air was warm and comfortable. The authorities distributed a small portion of bread and water to tide us over.

The next morning our train arrived. It was a nine day trip out to the west. We stopped in Poznan and were led off the train and into another Russian detention camp for processing. Russian troops interrogated each one of us and made sure our papers were in order. This is where Bruno and I parted ways. We gave each other a final hug and then he turned and disappeared. I never saw him again. I tried to remain calm because I was overcome by the thought that soon I would have the chance to disappear myself and end this sorry chapter of my life.

I remained at the camp for a few more days. The conditions were not much better than the previous two camps, but at least I was not required to do any labor. I received my dismissal papers on August first. When the documents were handed to me, I gazed down upon them to make sure this was really happening. On the dismissal stood my first name, last name, my home address on Kattan Street, and so on. Yes, that was really me!

The Russian transport leader wanted to maintain order among the excited collection of ex-prisoners so they made us march out in single file from the camp to the main railway station in Poznan. We were all very happy and hurried onto the train. We left Poznan at ten o'clock in the evening bound for Katowice. We arrived the next day at two o'clock in the afternoon. I was still wearing the German cap and uniform given to me for the propaganda event in Kiev but I still had the black Russian coat that I wore over the outfit. I got off the train, walked about five hundred meters out from the railway station and had a look around. I was feeling quite nervous as my moment of truth had come. There was a company of Polish soldiers at the station waiting to receive us. They were directed to bring the war prisoners to a different camp in Katowice for processing. It wasn't possible to process all of us in Poznan because it served as a very busy connection hub for thousands ex-prisoners traveling on to Danzig and Ostoberschlesien.

Many civilians were waiting at the train station to receive their loved ones. There were shouts of joy and people hugging each other, telling stories about what happened while we were away. Many of the former prisoners leaving the train started to run, as not to get caught up on the mass of humanity rushing to greet them. I wanted no part of this. I kept my head down and my black coat wrapped tightly around me as I slipped past the Polish soldiers waiting to process us. I hurried across the train tracks to get away from the scene. I could not risk them discovering that I was not in the Polish military.

I walked through Katowice towards the nearby town of Zabrze where I was born. Along the way I passed by several people in the streets, but tried to avoid eye contact. One woman, though, caught my attention as she walked toward me going in the opposite direction. She was my age and gave me a long look as I approached her. I gave her a slight smile. She may have noticed that I was wearing a military uniform but I'm guessing that she did not see it well enough to identify it as German. She stopped in front of me, reached into her purse and gave me ten zloty. "Here, you look hungry," she said.

It was a welcome gift as I did not have any money. I thanked her and continued own the main street through Zabrze toward the police station. I knew many of the people who worked there and believed I would find a sympathetic friend. As I got closer I caught the attention of a guard standing outside. "You!" he shouted. "Come over here. Right away!"

I hesitated for a brief moment then continued walking up to him as naturally and confidently as I could. Inside I was in a panic. It was a mistake to come here, I thought. My game was over. I'll be discovered and end up back in a Russian detention camp. I put my trust in God that he had guided me to the right place.

When I got closer he ordered, "Come, follow me."

I said nothing, following him into the police station, down the hall, and into a room where an officer sat behind a desk. "Have a seat" he said.

I sat in a chair on the other side of the desk and waited for my fate to be decided. The officer behind the desk looked up to attend to me and asked sternly "Can you speak Polish?"

I answered him almost arrogantly "Of course. Since I am a Polish citizen I must certainly also be able to speak Polish."

"May I see your papers?"

I reached into my pocket, careful not to expose the German uniform I was wearing, and handed him the documents I received for my release. The man behind the desk took his time to study them carefully. After a few minutes he seemed unsatisfied. He got up from his desk and said, "Wait here."

He walked into the hallway and talked with the guard that brought me inside, who was waiting just outside the office. The two of them spoke in a hushed tone. I could not make out what they were saying, but they made me believe that they may hold me here in custody again. I decided that it was time to call upon the sympathy of my plight.

"Excuse me, officers," I said aloud as to get their attention. "I am a Polish officer. I am returning from Russia, having spent the past two years in a prison camp. I have been released by the NKVD, and therefore I was officially released by the Russians. I'm tired. I'm filthy. I haven't had a decent meal in months. I haven't seen my family in years and they probably believe I'm dead. I just want to go home. Will you please help me?"

The officer from the desk lookup up at me and said "Right away, soldier." In an instant I was handed my release papers. Then he called for a nearby Polish corporal.

"Accompany this man to the trolley." he said to the corporal. "Do not ask him any further questions. We want him to return to his family as quickly as possible."

"Thank you so much," I said to both of them in my best weary voice. The two of us walked out of the building and a short distance down the street. We waited in silence for a few minutes until the trolley arrived. When the door opened the corporal stepped inside and told the conductor that I need not pay for my ride. The conductor nodded in agreement. I thanked both men as I boarded the trolley. There was yet a ray of hope for my safe return home.

As I sat on the trolley bench I began to worry about my German uniform. That was going to get me into trouble. I wondered if I would be able to exchange it for civilian clothes. Then I remembered that I have a cousin who lives in nearby Königshütte. I took the trolley for another five stops before hopping off to take a path through the fields to the town of Königshütte. By this time, it had become quite dark. It had been a long day. I laid down in a wheat field where I would catch some sleep and wait out the night.

The next morning I continued my walk down the between the fields until I reached the town of Königshütte. I walked silently through the streets careful to avoid making contact with anyone. When I finally arrived at my cousin's place, I looked around all sides of the house to make sure that no one would see me enter. I rapped on the door and waited impatiently. I felt fortunate that she answered the door herself. At first my cousin didn't recognize me. It was no wonder. I had lost quite a bit of weight over the past year or two. I was unshaven and very dirty. I told her that I hoped she can help me out quickly as I was in trouble and that I needed clothes. Then a warm smile came over her. She grabbed me by the arm dragging me inside before abruptly closing the door behind us. She told me that I first needed to rest, get a bath, shave, and then the next day I could be on my way. She would take care of everything for me. I was happy to oblige. I soon felt like a human again. I was extremely grateful for her hospitality.

Early the next morning I got back on the trail and my adventure continued. From Königshütte I boarded a bus using the few coins that my cousin had given me and traveled through the town of Hindenburg and on to Gleiwitz. I wanted to avoid the center of town because I had the feeling that I would be stopped and questioned. As I got off the bus, I found a police control station right in front of me. I called on God's help once again to get me past this. It certainly looked like I had fallen into a trap as I arrived. I ducked my head and made my way quickly through the side streets of my home town. As I walked, I took note of many things, unfamiliar faces, Russians, Poles, and houses that had been hit by Germans artillery fire. I had seen many images of the war, from the unpleasant to those things downright gruesome, but seeing the effects of the damage and the occupation in a place that was so familiar to me was very unsettling.

I walked a little further and there it was, my own house. But even that familiar place was not immune from the scars of war. There was a sign posted prominently on the side of the house that that read, "No Looting". I tried the front door but it was locked. I only took a quick look through the window in the front room so that no one would believe that I was trying to force my way inside. It appeared that no one was home. A feeling of anxiety rushed over me. I left my house and headed quickly for the center of town where some of my relatives lived. After a short walk, I saw my sister-in-law in the yard outside of her home. I ducked my head down to keep her from recognizing, me but she turned to look in my direction and it was too late. She shouted over and over "This can't be true!" as she ran toward me. She knew that I was missing since 1943 and assumed that I had been killed. Before she could throw her arms around me, I laid my finger on her mouth so that she would be still for a moment.

"I need to stay out of sight. Do you understand?"

"Oh, of course" she replied, but she was still very emotional. "Oh, Oskar!" She couldn't help herself and gave me a brief but very firm embrace. She took one step back but held on to my arm. "I can't believe it!"

I spoke to her calmly and slowly. "Where is my family? Are they alright?"

"They're both fine. They're home right now. Come, let's go."

She took my arm and led me down the road I had just come from back to my home. The front door was boarded up to deter people from looting, so we went around through the back of the house. When we arrived she casually knocked on the door. At that moment a young lad jumped up and ran over to us. He said, "I can open the door, Tanta, I have the key." I peered through the window into the house and saw the face of my son. At that moment I truly felt at home.

Chapter 16 IT'S NOT SAFE HERE

My son did not recognize me through the window. I think it was because I was wearing a Polish military uniform that my cousin had given me. My wife followed close behind him. She casually opened the door and looked at me. In an instant her expression changed to that of shock. The color drained from her face as she began to faint. I quickly put my arms around her and held her close.

"It's okay." I said. "Everything is going to be okay. I'm here now." My sister-in-law just beamed with joy. My son stayed quiet, waiting for his turn to greet me.

"Stay calm." I continued. "Let's go inside. I don't want people to see me." By this time my son, Heinz, put his arm around me as well. I held him tightly.

We took one step into the house before my wife sprang to life and pulled me back. "Oskar, wait, we can't go in."

"Why not?"

She hesitated before answering in a hushed tone "There is a Russian officer inside."

My feelings flipped from joy to anger very quickly. "What do you mean there's a Russian officer inside? What is a Russian officer doing in my house?" I brushed her aside and walked sternly through the door and into the living room. For a moment the three others waited behind me but soon followed.

The first person I saw was a woman. Her face looked familiar to me but I could not recall her name. I could tell that she was a German, though. Then I saw the Russian officer. At first he showed no interest, continuing his conversation with the German woman. I stood in the doorway and said nothing to them. Eventually I got the officer's attention. I realized then that I needed to stay calm and continue my deception in front of this 'Ivan'. The game was still on. He stood up and introduced himself and the woman he was with. I didn't retain their names, forgetting them just as quickly as they were uttered. I said 'hello' but did not offer my name. He must have sensed that I was in no mood for conversation with this intruder, as he soon announced that he needed to be going and left with the other woman. I was happy to see them leave. I was finally alone with my family. My wife explained that the German woman was a neighbor. She and the Russian soldier stopped by a short time ago to check on us.

Though the two had left there were still several others in the house. My mother-in-law and other in-laws were also there. They explained to me that the Poles coming into the area were driving many people out of their homes. My in-laws were victims of this. Still it was a joyful reunion. Relieved to be at last home with my family, I now had the opportunity to properly greet my wife and son and everyone else. There was so much to tell each other that we talked long into the night. We enjoyed each other's company so much. I told them all about my experiences and they shared their own struggles that they had to face. I understood clearly that, although the war was over, there were still many hardships to endure.

Eventually we were overcome by the need to get some sleep. I felt great joy and comfort being in my own bed with me wife beside me, though the sounds of war were still present. A few times during the night I heard cries of help in the neighborhood, from women who were being abused by Polish men who recently made their way into the neighborhood. I wanted so much for my ordeal to be over and to shut out those sounds, but I could not. The streets weren't safe, or at least they weren't safe for the Germans who lived here. The war wasn't over for me; it had only entered a new phase.

I hadn't yet checked in with the police, because from all I've learned since my return I wasn't sure if I should stay here. I had an uncle who lived nearby, and I believed that he may be able to explain to me what the situation was and give me advice as to what I should do. The next morning I walked to his house. As my aunt opened the door she was startled, not expecting to see me. She quickly brought me inside. My uncle was not at home. The news wasn't good. She told me that anyone who claimed to be former soldier but was caught without papers, would be immediately jailed. She also made it clear to me that my uncle could not help me, even though I had formal release papers from the Russian camp and from the Polish authorities in Zabrze.

When she told me this, I paused for a moment to reflect on how I should handle this. It was clear to me that I could not go back to the police. Many years ago I had helped my uncle out of a problem. I felt he would be willing to return the favor now. The fact that he could not, meant to me that the situation was very bad. I looked up at my aunt and told her that I could always turn to God for help.

My aunt was clearly uncomfortable at my presence in her house so I didn't stay much longer. I walked quickly through the streets back to my house. I explained to my family that we could not stay here. I felt that the best place for us was with my parents. I collected my belongings that my son hid under the floorboards. Together we gathered as much as we could carry and walked to the train station. As we left the house I looked back one last time, wondering if I would ever see it again. I felt sad to leave. I endured so much hardship just to survive long enough to have the chance to get back to that house, and yet after staying there only one day I was already leaving it behind.

We boarded the train heading west crossing the Oder River and along the Czechoslovakian border to Glaiz. On the train I spoke Russian to any Pole who approached me. I instructed the rest of my family not to say a word. There were two other Russian officers on board the train. I wanted the Poles to think I was one of those Russian guys and leave me alone. It worked. From Glaiz it was a short bus ride to Bad Kudowa. We arrived at my parents' home late in the evening. They lived in a large villa at the edge of a forest, very close the Czech border. It was on a hill overlooking the town below. When they opened the door for us they were shocked to see me, believing that I was missing in action. Inside the house, we exchanged stories again. I was saddened to learn that the situation in Bad Kudowa was the same as in Gleiwitz. It meant that I could not report to the police here either. We would all need to stay out of sight and away from the authorities until the danger had passed. We knew not how long that would be.

Safety became a big concern for us, but we soon had another. Food was scarce after the war and we had little means of procuring it. I could not walk openly into town to buy anything. It was also nearly impossible for me to get a job to support this large, extended family. There were now many mouths to feed. I needed to start looking for food and provisions. I woke up very early each morning and went out into the woods to find mushrooms. At night, I would walk through the fields and bring back potatoes, cabbage and kohlrabi that I had stolen. I did not feel shame; I did what I needed to do to survive. I had to bring back enough food to feed seven people.

A few days after we arrived at my parents' house, I treated them to a special surprise. I came home with a calf that I had purchased from the mayor of the town for one hundred and eighty zloty. Everyone was delighted except for my parents. They were uneasy about the thought of me out in the open market. The mayor believed I was Russian and sold me the calf without question. I believed I could pass as a Russian as I still shaved my head clean. It worked. It took us only half an hour to clean and prepare the calf. When it was ready and we enjoyed a very nice meal. I hadn't eaten like that in a long time and it felt very good to have a full belly.

The following day we were back to foraging for food, though the large meal from the day before brought us some much needed strength. This pattern of staying quiet and out of sight in the house by day and venturing out by night to find food continued for another fourteen days. Then things became much more difficult for us. We received a visit from the authorities declaring that the Polish government had seized my parent's house. Many Polish citizens had their land and their belongings confiscated by the government as the communist party began to assert itself.

My parents pleaded with the authorities to allow us to stay in the house until we could be re-settled. Fortunately for us they agreed. My parents informed the police that there were seven people living there: the two of them, my brother, my two sisters, a woman (my wife), and her son. I could not let it be known to anyone that I lived there, as I was not registered as a Polish citizen. I spent the daylight hours hiding in the woods. At night I would creep back into the house to bring back whatever food I could find and get some sleep. Then I would wake up very early the next morning to slither out of the house again.

One day while I was out my, parents did something that made me very uneasy. They befriended a new person in the neighborhood, a community worker who had moved in to house just a short distance from my parents' home toward the center of town. The man told my parents that he could hide some of their valuables for safekeeping. I'm not sure what he said to my parents, but it earned their trust. My parents had already lost their land and their home and they feared it would not be long before the communists came for the rest of their possessions. They were probably right, but I did not know enough about this man to believe he could be trusted.

My mother and father collected some jewelry and other personal belongings in a strong box and locked it. They encouraged me to do the same and I reluctantly agreed. They were excited about having met this guy as he made a very nice impression on them. I wished I could share their enthusiasm. That evening I accompanied my parents to the house where the man had agreed to meet us. Once we turned over the boxes I tried to make my way back home quickly, but the he encouraged us to stay and struck a conversation with my parents. I tried to say as little as possible. At one point one he promised my parents that he would barter with them, giving us provisions that he would get from Poland in return for items they would sell to him. That made me suspicious of this operation and from then on I was even less comfortable around him.

The next day this community worker came by the house to check on how they were doing, claiming to be concerned. At the time, I was away from the house in the forest. Somehow he persuaded my parents to come back to his place in the evening to show him what was in the box that he was hiding for them. I could not convince my mother that this was a bad idea, so my brother and I reluctantly accompanied my parents back to his place that evening to unlock the box and show him. When we got there he sat us down at the kitchen table, while he disappeared in to the basement to retrieve the box. He emerged a short time later with the item and sat it on the table. Then he looked up, gazed at all of us asked me who I was. I would not answer him, but my mother explained that I was her son. He gave me an odd look. Then he pulled out his cigarette case and offered one to my father and brother, but he closed the case in front of me without offering me one. I got the message.

My mother opened the box and explained what was inside. She felt compelled to go into details and proudly talked about the history of some of the objects. The man did his best to convey a sense of interest, but said very little. He peered carefully in the box at its contents, making a mental note of everything inside. When the tour was finished he thanked us and made it clear that we should be on our way.

The next day I was up again before the sun came out to spend the day in the forest. The areas I frequented were becoming less abundant. It was increasingly difficult for me to find food by scavenging in the woods and creeping around farms at night. This practice was clearly not sustainable. I needed to earn some money in order to put food on the table for my family. The next morning I braved the light of day and walked to the nearby village of Jerzykowice to look for work. At the edge of town, I walked up to a farm house. There was an old man outside repairing a door. I approached him and asked if he could offer me any work. His name was Draschner. I was happy when he agreed to hire me as a farm hand. This would be a big help for our family.

While I was able to earn a little money from my work at the farm, my mother began to trade some of their possessions with the community worker whom she trusted with our belongings. That also helped put food on the table, but over time she received less and less in return. It got to the point where the only thing the man would give us in return for a piece of jewelry was a half of a kilogram of salt. My mother felt she had no choice but to accept whatever he would offer as we had few other options to get food.

My job at the farm made me feel more confident being outside in the daylight hours, so I spent less time hiding in the woods and more time helping out around the house when I wasn't needed on the farm. Around eleven o'clock one afternoon I was chopping wood outside of my parents' home, when something caught my attention. I looked out toward the town and noticed the community worker leave his house. An hour later, I saw him return but he was not alone. Three soldiers followed close behind and they were headed toward our villa. I dashed inside to alert my parents. I realized that I needed to get everything out of the house that was already packed up, but it was too late for that. There was just enough time to warn them and to run out into the woods and hide myself.

My family huddled inside hoping that this confrontation would not drive them out of their home. The soldiers entered the house without knocking at the door with the gentleman that my parents trusted following close behind. My mother pleaded with them to leave our family alone, but the soldiers did not react to anything she said. While two of the soldiers searched the house one of them ordered my mother to tell them where she had hidden her belongings, as they were being confiscated by the State. She was too upset to answer, so the men proceeded to turn the entire house upside down. They knocked on all the walls and the floorboards searching for valuables and weapons. It wasn't long before they discovered a trunk that we had packed and promptly confiscated it. They also took a few other items they felt had some value including those that my wife and child had brought with us. They left with their loot, but did not appear to be satisfied. I watched them carefully from a safe distance in the shadows of the forest, waiting for them to get far enough away from the house before going back inside. I had a feeling they would return.

I needed to make sure that my own belongings were safe from the communists. The next day I walked down to the community worker's house and demanded that he return my own belongings. I was surprised that he complied, but he conveyed a rather smug attitude as if to let me know that he would get them back eventually. I brought them to the farm house in Jerzykowice for safe keeping. I was grateful to the farmer for allowing me to hide my belongings there. I did not stay long, nor did I return there to do any work for a few days. I felt it would be risky for me to be seen there, at least not right away. I didn't want to put the farmer in danger of getting involved with me, but my options were becoming quite limited and we were running out of food.

Such encounters were becoming more commonplace. The authorities continued to search through houses in town, even at night. Fortunately for me, the weather was nice and it allowed me to spend the nights in the woods. One afternoon the police returned to my parents' house, just as I expected. I knew they were not satisfied with the items they took from us the first time. This time they meant business. The police rummaged through the house again, flipping over furniture and knocking holes in the walls as they searched for anything of value. They were also intent on capturing me, an undocumented civilian who could pose a threat to the government. They demanded to know where I was, but my family continued to deny that there was anyone else living there. The situation escalated when one of the officers pulled out a pistol and pointed it at my mother and father. He announced to them "If the rest of your valuables and your fugitive son are not back in this house by nine o'clock tonight you know what will happen to you." With that, the officers left the house. My boy ran to find me in the woods and brought me the news. I knew I had to act right away.

Chapter 17 AUF WIEDERSEHEN

We needed to leave immediately. I placed my trust in a Czech I knew who lived near the border, which was very close to my parents' home in Bad Kudowa. I gathered up my loved ones: my parents, wife, son, brother, two sisters, and my four year old nephew. We took with us only a few items, some clothing, a few pots to cook with, and whatever money we still had. We left the family house on the hill and hiked into the woods. We walked to within five hundred meters of the border crossing and took cover. I instructed everyone to lay low and not say a word while I continued on to make sure the rest of the way to the crossing was clear. It was. I motioned to them that the path was safe. Then we all made a dash for Czech territory.

We continued on through the forest to the home of the Czech man that I knew. He lived with his wife who was German. He was happy to help and offered us a small room in the house where my family could stay for a while. I could tell that he had done this many times before. I left my family there and headed back that night to Jerzykowice to retrieve my belongings. My family was deeply concerned for my safety and worried sick over me until I got back. I returned later that evening without incident. We huddled together in that one room plotting what our next move would be.

We knew that we were not out of danger here. The border patrol would often come by and search the place. I needed to find other options. The next morning I returned to Bad Kudowa to see what was happening at my parents' house. When I got close to the house I stayed hidden in the woods and observed some activity from a safe distance. I could see men in the house and in the surrounding area. They were Polish authorities and they were clearly searching for us. I stayed and watched for a while before returning to the house over the border.

Ten days had past. We knew it was time to leave. If we stayed any longer, we would risk being captured. I determined that my best course of action for us would be to make our way to Germany, but our first task was to get away from the house. I needed some time to prepare for the journey. The nine of us crossed back into Polish territory to find new places to hide. Our first stop was the farm house in Jerzykowice. I asked farmer Draschner if he would permit my wife and son to stay on the farm for a few days. He was understanding and happy to help us. Then I led my parents and siblings back to Bad Kudowa to stay with other friends we had there. We did our best to convey our gratitude.

On October fifth, the Polish government announced that all Germans living in Poland who wished to return to Germany would be allowed to register for a transport to take them there. My parents and siblings took advantage of this opportunity and signed up for the transportation. That would not take place for some time, but I was relieved that they would soon be free from their troubles here. I was not as fortunate. As a former soldier in the German army, I was concerned about what might happen to me if I were to approach the Polish authorities so my family and I remained hidden in Jerzykowice. We relocated my wife and son to a different house, an acquaintance of mine also in Jerzykowice who was kind enough to help. I remained on the farm to earn a little more money. I also felt it was safer for them to be separated from me.

That decision proved to be a good one. On November first a group of five men, each carrying arms, approached the farm to give notice that the property was being seized by the government. At the time, I was working in the potato fields together with the farmer and a few other farm hands. A woman ran out to bring us the news. I accompanied the farmer back to the house to see what was happening, but the farmer stopped short of the house and gestured to me to continue on alone. As I got close to the house, five men came out from around the corner and stood before me. One of them asked sharply, "Are you the owner of this house?"

"No, I only work here." I replied to the officers in Polish. That seemed to surprise him.

"Who are you then?" asked another.

"I am a Czech, but that I can speak Polish. What is the problem, officers?"

"Never mind that," said the first one. "Show me your papers."

"My papers are in the farm house, but the house is locked. Everyone is working out in the fields."

The men looked at each other and smirked. One of the officers held up his badge. "We are with the criminal police. Raise your hands and turn around."

I complied. The officer frisked me, looking for weapons. Of course he found none. He spun me around and said, "Oh, it's you, the Partisan that escaped from Kudowa."

"I am no Partisan!" I replied strongly. "I'm just a worker here."

They weren't buying it. The officer with the badge said, "Come with me." and reached to take my arm.

I remained calm in an attempt to convey a sense of confidence and innocence. I took a step back and said, "Look, please, just allow me get into the house to fetch my coat and my papers. Then I'll be happy to go with you and we can clear this whole thing up. Okay?" I was making a play for time as, of course, there were no such papers.

After an uneasy pause, the oldest of the policemen looked at the two officers to his right and ordered, "Escort this man inside".

I smiled back. "Thank you, officer." I turned my back to them and walked up to the front door with the two policemen following close behind. When I got to the house, I stopped and turned abruptly as one of the men bumped into me.

"Oh, I forgot. The house is locked. I can't go in this way." I looked around the house while the men stared at me. I pointed to the hayloft over the barn. "There it is. I can get into the house through the hayloft. Help me find a ladder."

I looked around the stable, but could not find one. The two men made a half-hearted attempt to help me look, but appeared to be more interested in getting to the end of this exercise so they could arrest me. I walked back out of the stable and stood for a while staring at the hayloft, which was the only solution I could come up with for getting out of this latest predicament. There was a door to the barn that looked like it was just tall enough for me to climb up and reach the hayloft. I stepped on the door handle and reached for the top of the door. The tallest policeman helped me by holding the door steady. It took some effort, but I was able to reach the hayloft above and pull myself up. I rolled over and slowly got to my feet. I looked down at the men staring back up at me. I smiled back and called to them, "Auf Wiedersehen!" Then I scampered into the house as quickly as I could.

Once I got inside, I felt a bit safer. It would buy me a little time to think of a way out of this. The house was locked but that wasn't the only thing keeping the authorities from entering. I listened to them shout at each other and learned that they were too afraid to attempt to break in, fearing that I may have picked up a gun from the house. I walked down the stairs and into the kitchen, found my coat and put it on. I peeked outside and saw that the policemen had surrounded the house. One of them shouted to me "Come out at once or we'll burn the house down!" I thought about it for a while and concluded they wouldn't burn the house down just to force me out. Then I came up with a plan.

I walked through the house to make sure that all of the windows around the yard were locked. There were now only four men, as one of them left to get reinforcements. They held their pistols in the air and ordered me again to come out. I answered "Okay, you have me. I'll come out. Please don't shoot!" I believed that offered me a few more minutes to get this right.

I walked to a window by the side of the house that overlooked the garden. It was one that I had locked before but this time I looked out and observed that side of the house was unguarded for the moment. I quickly jerked open the window. It was old and I broke one of the panes. I began to climb out, but got my foot stuck in the curtain. I shook my foot to free myself and tore the fabric as I tumbled out of the window. I didn't fall far but I hit the ground hard and rolled down a bank into a deep drainage ditch. I crawled through the ditch as quickly as I could until I reached a short path through the field which led into the woods. As the forest was close to the Czech border, it would not be difficult to make my escape from there.

I got to my feet and without looking back I ran as fast as I could. My eyes were fixed on the wooded area in front of me, still about three hundred meters away. I was expecting to hear the whistle of bullets fired in my direction reminding me of the time we charged into Kiev, all the while hoping that this would not end up being a foolish decision. I was excited when I reached the first trees in the forest. I ducked behind the largest of them, hunching over to catch my breath. A minute later, I turned back to look at the house. All four men were lurking around the property, waiting for me to make my appearance. They eventually came to the side of the house where I made my escape and discovered the broken window. They knew then that I was gone.

For a moment I enjoyed listening to them cuss at each other. Then I walked back toward the house to make myself visible at the edge of the forest. I wanted them to know that I was no longer in the building so that they wouldn't think of trying to burn down the house, but I was still far enough away so that they could not shoot me. Eventually one of the officers spotted me. They quickly left the farm and disappeared. Perhaps they didn't pursue me, because they thought I would bring other Partisans out of the woods to join me.

I remained in the cover of the forest for the rest of the day and spent the night there again under clear skies. I was convinced that those men would soon return with reinforcements and turn over the entire village to apprehend me. My wife and son were safely tucked away in a schoolhouse where a teacher that we knew well was helping them stay out of sight. I found a hiding place on the hill overlooking the town. I made myself a bunker of sorts, drawing on the skills I had learned from the Ukrainian officers several years before, who made such marvelous and well-hidden shelters. I stayed on the hill for a few days alone, waiting for the danger to subside.

Chapter 18 FOOD AND SHELTER

The farmer in Jerzykowice and I had become friends. He was sympathetic to the problems I faced and did his best to help. From time to time he visited me, bringing me things to eat and keeping me company, but this didn't last long. Although the farmer was a respected person in the community and even a party member, the authorities were suspicious of him. They suspected he was aiding the Partisan movement. Over time the farmer learned that he was being watched, so he stopped coming to visit me. After eight days on the hill, I decided to make my way back into Bad Kudowa. I was beginning to worry about my family. I walked back to the farmhouse that night to visit the farmer. He was kind enough to give me some bread, flour, vegetables, and potatoes. I would then commute into town to distribute the food to the buildings where my family members were hiding out. From time to time, I would return to the farmer for more food and make my rounds again.

This continued for about a week, before even this source of food came to an end. One day while in my hideout on the hill, farmer Draschner came up to visit me. It was a surprise for me, as he had not come this way in quite some time. At first I was happy to see him, but quickly learned that he quite upset. He told me that the Polish government seized not only his land, but also his farm house. He tearfully explained that he was no longer able to afford me even a small piece of bread, as he had none for himself. He had lost his home and his means of supporting himself, and fell into despair. I hugged him and promised that I would do my best to take care of him as well.

We stayed together for a long while, not saying much but indeed grateful for each other's company and sympathy. Then I remembered that several weeks earlier the two of us had hidden an emergency stash of food up here. We had buried three crates of potatoes and a crate of kale, carrots, cabbage, and other vegetables. Smiles rushed over our faces. With great excitement, we dug up the crates and discovered that the food was in excellent condition. This lifted his spirits and bought us some time. I left to collect my family members. Draschner did the same, setting out in a different direction to gather four other families that had helped us along the way. A few hours later, we assembled on the hill. Together we peeled potatoes and rutabagas to make ourselves something to eat. We were hungry and homeless, but we found a way to turn the event into a party of sorts.

Throughout Poland there was widespread hunger after the war. Food was scarce. Polish citizens who were properly registered were given a card that allowed them to receive basic rations of food, but even those did not go far to feed a family. Those who did not register with the authorities did not receive this card. Unregistered people could still request a food subsidy, but they were forced to work for the Polish government without compensation for two days before they received anything at all, not so much as a piece of bread.

As for our family, we looked good but we had no strength. We were living on three potato pancakes in the afternoon, and in the evening we had a thin soup with flour, but without any meat or fat or protein of any kind. It wasn't long before our supply was running low. Once again we needed to come up with a better solution.

I weighed my options and I decided to travel to Braunau in the Sudetenland. There, I would seek guidance from an uncle of mine who lived there. He was a leader in the anti-fascist movement. I thought it may be possible to go through Czechoslovakia and from there, make our way to the American-controlled zone. I wanted to consult with him to find out how we could go about this. My seventeen year old son asked to go with me and I was happy to have his company.

At four o'clock in the morning of November twenty-first, the two of us set out for the Czech boarder. I had learned that the border police did not arrive until six o'clock and before then the crossing was unguarded. We made it to within two hundred meters of the boarder and then stopped. I put my hand on his shoulder. Quietly I instructed him "This is how it's going to work. I will walk ahead about fifty meters. You stay right here. Do not let me out of your sight. You got that?"

"Yes, Papa," he answered nervously.

"If at any time you feel that there was any danger you turn around and run back to the house where you and your mother are staying. Stay on this path, do not look around, and run as fast as you can. Understand?"

"Yes."

"If something happens to me do not worry. I will find a way to escape and come back for you."

Heinz nodded nervously in agreement.

I stood up and crept slowly towards the crossing, my eyes fixed on the guard house. When I reached the point of being fifty meters in front of my son I heard the sound of someone coming upon me very fast. I turned around and saw my son bounding toward me in a complete panic. When he reached me I put my arms around him, pulled him off to the side and dragged him to the ground. Gasping for air he explained "Papa, there are people coming! I heard footsteps!"

I tried to keep him quiet. "It's okay, just calm down. Where did you hear them?"

"I heard footsteps coming down the same path that we took."

I held him tightly. "Shhh, it's alright. We'll be fine so long as we stay quiet." I poked my head up and looked all around the woods in every direction but it was hard to see anything.

"Do you see something?" he asked.

"No, nothing." I continued to scan the area.

"I hear it! They're getting closer!" Heinz put his head down.

Still holding onto him I said quietly "Nothing is going to happen to you. I promise." I cupped my ears to try and make out more clearly what it was, but all I could hear was the sound of my son's heart beating so loudly in his chest it seemed like it would burst out of him.

We stayed low to the ground in silence for a few minutes. Once his breathing slowed to a normal pace he picked his head up and looked around. "I don't hear it anymore. The sound is gone."

I could tell that he felt ashamed. I stroked his hair and told him "Look, it's alright. I know exactly what you heard. It is nothing to be concerned about. Okay?"

"Okay. I'm okay now."

I whispered, "Follow me." I looked into his eyes and gave him a reassuring wink. His face brightened and we stood up. The guard house was indeed empty and the crossing clear. After a few steps, we were across the border and on Czech soil. We were proud of our accomplishment, but knew we were far from being out of danger. Our path took us into the town of Hronov. We knew there were Czech border patrols that were present on the streets of these villages and were careful not to run into any. We turned north and hiked to the town of Politz. There we noticed a border patrolman who was definitely staring at us. We pretended that we were not together, as one of us walked about a hundred meters in front of the other. It wasn't long before the patrolman lost interest in us and we made it through the city unnoticed.

Our travel took us through the town of Labnay towards Stern. I was not familiar with the area so I had to consult a map that we had found. We reached the main church in Stern and figured out what direction to go to get to Braunau. We found a path that took us there. As we walked I noticed there were fresh footprints and dog tracks on the ground. We had to be careful not to fall into the hands of the border patrol, so we scrambled up the mountain above the path to walk parallel to it. As we climbed, we heard the sound dogs barking. I turned to Heinz and said to him, "We're in danger. We need to find a different way to get there, something that keeps us away from the border."

We climbed back down the mountain and found a different path that seemed to take us further west, deeper into Czech territory. We followed that until we arrived at a building called the "Amerika Inn." Once again, I felt that God had guided my way and saw to it that I did not run into any guards. Since we were without papers, we would have been considered illegal migrants and that would not have been good. We met an old man who appeared to be unthreatening. We asked him for directions to Braunau and he was happy to help. From the inn, we stayed on the same path. It meandered through fields of wheat and vegetables until we found ourselves in the village of Weckelsdorf. We continued on and it wasn't long before we at last reached the walls that surround the town of Braunau. Heinz had been to my uncle's house before and was somewhat familiar with the area. We made our way quickly around the town square, and before we knew it we were standing in front of the house. My uncle came to open the door. He took one look at me and was in such a shock that he needed to sit down. He couldn't believe it was possible that we had arrived here. Once safely inside, he gave us something to eat. We told him all about our journey here and how we evaded the security presence in this area. He was amazed by our perseverance and good fortune.

We stayed there for only one day and night. That's because the authorities in town searched each house three times a week looking for illegal refugees. It was nice to spend time with my uncle, but I learned that there would be no route to the west through Czech territory for us. We needed to find a different way. When it was time to leave he gave us each one loaf of bread for the trip. We took the same way back home that we took getting there. We were very careful not be caught by the border guards. After six hours, we were back at the border. This time there were Polish patrolmen stationed at the crossing. We stayed a safe distance away in the woods, waiting for the shift to end before dashing across. We continued on the path through the woods and reached Bad Kudowa. I accompanied my son back to where my wife was staying and told her what I had learned. There were no solutions yet in sight, but still plenty of other adventures waiting for me.

Chapter 19 ESCAPE

Life for us went on as it did before with all the excitement, commotion and hardship. I continued to hide my wife and son in one location while I sought refuge in other places, doing what I could to feed those I cared for. Winter was upon us. Food was even harder to come by as the crops had all been harvested. There was no farm work to be had. I spent my days searching for any odd job I could find that would pay me a few coins. Sometimes I slept in a shed or a barn. For a while, I found shelter in the basement of a house that I was able to quietly get into. I couldn't stay in any one place for long, as I would risk being discovered.

One night I had stayed in a shelter with a group of community workers. It offered me a bed and meal consisting of thin soup and a small piece of bread. It was ten o'clock at night when we heard banging on the door. Before anyone could respond, the door burst open without warning. It was another Polish raid. They were quite common and unforgiving. Four men in uniform stormed inside to search the house. They plundered everything of value they could find. The oldest man in the house was ordered to accompany them to open the doors to all of the rooms. Every person they encountered was required to show their identification papers. As they got closer to the room I was sleeping in, I heard one of the officers asking the old man about me and give my description. When I heard that I quickly opened the nearest window and without hesitation jumped out. It was four and a half meters down to the ground, but it was better than being caught. I landed in some bushes which helped to break my fall. Luckily, I was not injured. I remained motionless, waiting to hear if anyone would look outside.

Staying in the room with me were several people including the twelve year old daughter of the family that owned the place. From the ground I looked up and saw her close the window behind me. I remained hidden in the bushes along a creek that ran close to the house. The night was very dark. It was very cold, but I stayed down there for a long time until I finally heard the police leave the house. I crept back inside, believing the danger had passed. I settled back into my bed and tried to fall back asleep, but I would get no more rest this night. Two hours later the ordeal repeated itself, as the police showed up again. I believe someone must have seen me re-enter the house and alerted the authorities. There were only two officials this time. The claimed that they returned to retrieve an accordion that they remembered seeing under a bed while they were here two hours earlier. I don't know if they were really that petty, or if that was just a story they told to make one more attempt to apprehend me. I remained motionless and silent in the bed, but no one entered the room. I heard the men leave after only a few minutes.

It was clear to me that the people who lived in the house were now afraid. I told the woman who owned that house that she should not let on that I was here. I felt badly for the people who were here, believing that I may have put them in danger because of my presence. I gathered the few items I had and left soon thereafter, allowing enough time for the officials to put some distance between them and the house. I spent the rest of the night walking around the woods, keeping away from the houses in town.

The next day I moved to another house in Bad Kudowa that was owned by the wife of a salesman. I knew the family, but not well. I discovered that I could find no rest there either, as I was betrayed by a neighbor who alerted the authorities of my presence. One day around noon, a policeman and a civilian approached the saleswoman. This time, I did not have an opportunity to escape. The house was on the main road. It had a store front facing the street with the living quarters in the back. I was helping the woman in the store with some cleaning and organizing to earn my stay. I walked to the front of the store just as the men entered. We immediately made eye contact with each other. I smiled then casually turned around to walk toward the back but they would not let me go so quickly.

The policeman said to me, "You. Come back here. Are you the owner of this place?"

I answered them in German, "No, I only work here. I will go get the owner."

There were several packages of advertising material in the front of the store. The two men focused their attention on that. The distraction gave me an opportunity to slip out the back door. The woman entered the store from the living area upon hearing the two men speak to me. She walked right past me to approach them. I reached down and grabbed a pail of water, as if it were part of the task that I was focused on and carried it out the door and into the yard. Once I was outside, I jumped over the fence and ran into the forest. After I was safely hidden, I turned to observe the house. I saw that it was being thoroughly searched. The woman was calling for me, but I stayed in the woods.

An hour later I felt the danger had subsided, so I returned to the house. The woman greeted me at the door with a puzzled look and asked me what that was about. I told her if something like this were to happen again, just tell the people that I am a neighbor. She was clearly uneasy about me being there and so once again it was time for me to leave. By nightfall, I finished the chores she had given me. I thanked her for her hospitality and left.

By cover of night, I walked to the village of Jerzykowice. The farmer Draschner owned a second farm in the village. There was a loft in that farmhouse that was uninhabited. I decided to find shelter there. When I got to the farmhouse, I saw that it was empty. The door was open, so I walked right in. It was dark, but I had been there before so I knew my way around. I climbed up into the attic and over onto the hayloft, then down a few stairs to a small room. I tried to open the door to the room, but the latch was jammed. I had a knife on me and I used it to pry the door open. I pushed it open slowly, just a few centimeters, and felt warm air coming from the room. There was a fire burning in the stove. Someone was inside.

I hesitated for a moment. I heard no other sounds coming from the room. With the door slightly open I shouted, "Come out of there or I will shoot!" although I did not have a weapon with me. I heard the floor boards creak as someone slowly got up from a chair and walked to the door. There was a rap on the wall as if someone had removed something. Was it a gun? Perhaps issuing a threat wasn't such a good idea. Thoughts raced quickly through my mind, as I tried to figure out a way to defend myself if I were attacked, but there was no time. Suddenly the door opened wide and a man stood before me wielding an axe. I put my arms up to my, face but by the light of the fire I saw that it was the farmer. He recognized me right away. "Oskar! I'm so happy to see you!" He put his axe down and we hugged each other. "We nearly had quite an accident here, didn't we?"

I breathed a sigh. "Yes, we sure did."

"Come inside and get warm."

I walked in and he quickly closed the door behind me. We shared storied that were eerily similar. He told me that he was also being pursued by the authorities. I explained to him why I had to leave Bad Kudowa and that I was being hunted down as well. The farmer told me he, too, was betrayed by a neighbor who reported him for assisting undocumented fugitives. The neighbor was so belligerent that one day he walked on to the farm, approached the farmer, and without a word just punched him and walked away.

We spent the next two days together in the loft at the farm. They were quiet days, something I hadn't experienced in some time. By that time, I assumed that my family's supplies were running low. It was time to procure some more food for them. I walked back down the mountain to Bad Kudowa to find my relatives and check on their situation. They were indeed quite hungry. I felt my best option was to bring something back from Czechoslovakia. Conditions there, however, had deteriorated. The border was now heavily guarded and they were not letting anyone into Nachod to bring food back into Poland. Food had become scarce in Czechoslovakia as well.

The trek over the border was now a very risky journey. If you were captured by the patrols they would confiscate everything you had and lock you up in jail for ten hours. I also heard that prisoners were beaten by the guards. They said that women received fifty lashes and the men received one hundred. After that, you were free to go. But the hunger was so great, that many people tried to do this in spite of the danger. Some who crossed the border made it all the way to Glatz, but if those who were caught there were terribly mistreated. One person we met returned from a prison and told us stories of how they would cut off the fingers of the Germans that they caught. The prisoner would place their fingers in a door and the thugs would slam the door closed on them.

Believing I had no better option, I set out for the border in spite of the warnings. I made my way down a path to the town of Zarech. There I hoped to acquire a card that would allow me to receive rations. Then my plan was to walk ten kilometers to Nachod, where I would purchase the goods. Around three o'clock in the afternoon, I set out for the border. I needed to reach it by midnight, because that was when the border patrols were relieved.

The crossing went smoothly. I safely reached the town of Zarech, but was disappointed to find that I was unable to receive a card for provisions because I could not claim any Czech heritage. I pressed on toward Nachod, where I did manage to purchase some food with the money I had earned. I was lucky to make it back across the border with my goods, and happy that I was able to provide for the people I was looking after.

I made several more trips this way into Czechoslovakia to bring back food over the next few months. This cycle continued until March thirteenth, 1946, when the Polish government organized a transport of the Germans living in the area back into German territory. The elderly and those with children were required to go to the Russian-controlled zone. Once there, the children through age fourteen and women through age forty were sent to a refugee camp. We decided that wasn't a good option for us. The last place I wanted to be was in a Russian camp.

We packed up what few belongings we still had and together as a family crossed the border back into Czechoslovakia. We were joined by several other people in this journey, including four children. Our destination was Nachod. One of the people in our group knew someone there who could provide us with shelter and some food for a few days.

Another person in our group told us she had a brother-in-law in Braunau. After a few days in Nachod, we pressed on further into Czech territory and into the town of Braunau. Her brother-in-law was kind and also allowed us to stay for a few days. He was on the Glazer committee and active in the anti-fascist movement. The woman with her children decided to remain in Braunau with her brother-in-law, leaving our group down to six people. She promised me that she would speak with her brother-in-law about getting me papers. The woman made good on her promise. Her brother-in-law instructed someone to drive me to Prague, where I could obtain a repatriation license for five hundred Kroner. We had just enough money with us to purchase this. The trip and the transaction were both successful, and soon I was on my way back to Braunau with papers in hand that afforded me the ability to travel freely across Czechoslovakia. I sat silently in the car in amazement that I was no longer an undocumented fugitive. The feeling of freedom washed over me. There were many obstacles yet to overcome. My family was still homeless, hungry, and I was without a means of supporting them. But no longer would I be hunted down like a dog, fearful of the glance of every stranger on the street.

Five adventurous years had come to an end. They were full of combat, despair, and hunger, but most of all deception. I am proud of what I had accomplished. I survived. Every day was a struggle to stay hidden and unknown. None of people I met, not even the NKVD ever learned who I really was. To everyone I met I was content to be simply known as "the man in the black fur coat".

CONCLUSION

I mentioned in the Introduction the journal is in surprisingly good condition. It is self-titled in the first four lines:

> 1941-1945 Bad-Kudowa, February 10, 1946
> The Man in the Black Fur Coat
> Adventures from the Russian military campaign
> from June 22, 1941 to July 1945

Oskar launches right into the marching orders to cross the Bug River from Poland into Russian territory to begin Operation Barbarossa. There is no back story; it is simply an account of his experiences during that period. The context of what his life was like before the war is noticeably absent, and as such the tale lacked a human element that I felt would have made it more interesting and personal. Other than the account of his adventures, there is very little attention given to what he was feeling or thinking, and very few details of the places he had been to and the people he had met. Many of the characters in the story didn't even have a name. I don't even know his wife's name, as he never mentioned it.

One place in his journal that stands out to me, is in the beginning of chapter three when he writes that he was given some vacation time, and in the next sentence he's already headed back to the front line. There isn't a word of his time at home or even where that home was. How did he feel being there and away from the combat? What did he do? What were his thoughts about the war and of what he had seen? I find it odd that he would choose to omit that. Perhaps he did not mean for this to be too much like a diary, or maybe he assumed that everyone would already know his back-story.

The structure of the document is also interesting. The journal consists of one hundred and seventeen handwritten pages. There are no paragraph breaks at all. The first eighty-one pages are written as if they were done in one sitting. It is in the Sütterlin style in black ink. Half way through page eight-two the handwriting style changes. It now in a recognizable script alphabet and the ink is blue. The handwriting is also much different; it looks clearly like it was written by someone else at a different time. The writing and the ink change again on page one hundred and two and remain that way to the end.

The story is also broken into pieces. In the "Sütterlin section" the story continues in a straight account up until his time in the NKVD camp. Shortly after the first handwriting change the writer seems to bring the story to a quick end, leaving the POW camp and seeing his son's face for the first time. This went on for only a few pages. After that, the story goes back to Oskar's time in the camp and adds more narrative about his experiences there. It's as if he realizes he had more of a tale to tell, or perhaps more time to tell it. When he reaches the encounter with his wife and son he picks up the story again from that point and tells about his struggles after his release in post-war Poland.

I say "the writer" because I believe that someone else was writing the story for him while he dictated it because of the change in writing style and ink. There is also another telling sign. In the Sütterlin section he spelled his parents' home town "Bad Kudowa", but in the other writing style it is spelled "Bad Cudova".

One of the most challenging tasks was the translation of the towns he noted when writing about the battles, troop movements, and places in Silesia. These were phonetically-spelled German understanding of the names of Ukrainian, Polish, and Czech towns. Many times I could tell that he just guessed at the name of the town. Often it was close but sometimes it was a mile off and a few were just plain unrecognizable. It is also common for the names of the towns to be quite different between German, Polish, Russian, Czech, and Ukrainian languages. It is also true that names of some of the towns within a language changed during the twentieth century. I did the best I could using maps and other accounts of the Eastern campaign, but I still wish I could have precisely identified all of them.

The timing of the story tells a lot about what was going on. On the first page he starts with February 10, 1946. The section after he went back to tell more stories of the prison camp, before he picked up the story after he got home, was dated March 12, 1946. This was only about a month after starting the story. During this period he was in Poland hiding from the authorities and looking after his family. There were long stretches of time where he had nothing to do but to stay hidden. I surmise that he reflected on his experiences and took the opportunity afforded to him to write it all down. That's why I started the story off in the way that I did.

The final section, representing his time in Poland after the war, was dated April 8, 1954. It was written two years after his arrival in the United States, and right around the time that he met my great aunt, Hedy. I believed that perhaps Hedy helped him write this portion of his journal. When I compared the handwriting to letters sent to me by my Aunt Hedy, I determined that the passages were not written by her.

The original story as I described above is quite dry, a series of events with little given to how Oskar was feeling or perceiving the world. The journal entries were recorded as if they were a report he was compelled to hand over to his commanding officer at the end of the day. There were moments in his story when he did go into some depth, but most of it was quite flat. I share his story in this book with some added measure of color and life to those places where it was noticeably absent. My sincerest intention is to present this as close to the truth as possible. How knowable is the truth? It is difficult to say. I can find no person alive today who can independently verify the events he describes, though I was able to correlate the dates and places of the battles he participated in. Without independent corroboration, I recognize that it is difficult for me to declare with certainty that this as a factual account. I know only what was written in the journal.

Once I completed the straight translation, I added some layers of character and depth. I did not deviate from the way he told his story or the sequence of events, nor did I add new characters or interactions with people that he did not describe. My goal is to stay true and accurate to his journal so that this history may be best preserved, but also to share his story in an honest and compelling way. For this advice I wish to thank a personal friend of mine who is a professor of creative writing at a major university in Massachusetts, describing this approach as "creative nonfiction".

If you are interested in the original "straight" translation, the transcribed German text, and even the original journal scans for research I can provide that as well. I have established a web site "www.theblackfurcoat.com" to support this project, and you may contact me through that site. You may also reach me via two popular social media sites where I maintain an active account.

There are a few gaps in the back story that I really wish I could fill in. It would greatly help me understand the context of what was happening. My biggest question is how Oskar came to the area he describes as his German home in the first place. He had a house in Gleiwitz where his wife and son lived, his parents owned a home in Bad Kudowa, and he had many relatives in that surrounding towns. It was the territory that is known as Lower Silesia. The story inspired me to find out more about this region of Poland. I learned that this land was settled by many Germans in the late nineteenth and early twentieth centuries during the German eastern expansion. Poland took back this area as part of the "Reclaimed Territories" following the war. I concluded that was why Oskar considered himself a German at heart yet lived in what became Polish territory. It is evident that he was not the only one in this situation. He mentions on a few occasions how Polish officers seem to be often associated with the German army.

I do not know when he joined the German Wehrmacht but he clearly felt that was where he belonged. He was a German through and through. There is a telling part of the story when he is sent to the POW camp and writes that hearing the Germany language spoken again brought a tear to his eyes.

One thing that puzzled me was how easy it was for Oskar to "flip sides" in the NKVD camp and go from being a "suffering prisoner" to a leadership position in the camp. Was justice that arbitrary in Russia? It was odd to me that the Russians were so quick to accept a Polish officer working on their side, especially one that was just brought in as a political prisoner. Though he did not go into detail how that happened, I guessed that the Russian army was thinned by the great losses they suffered in their struggle against the German push eastward. The Russians may have taken advantage of Oskar's availability to add to their ranks in what was a relatively low-risk situation for them.

There is another twist to the story concerning his arrival in the United States. My mother told me that she had heard Oskar was fleeing from Germany because he may have had ties to the Nazi party, though I have never found any evidence of this, nor did Oskar ever write about politics. It is clear that he was also leaving his wife. She also shared with me that his son severed ties with Oskar when he left, and would not speak with him again. If his son, Heinz, or any of his children are alive today I would very much like to meet them. The ship's manifest from his emigration in early 1952 shows that he arrived with a woman named Emma Scheja who was listed as his thirty-seven year old wife. My mother tells me that Emma was not his wife, but a family friend who agreed to the marriage in order to help him get into the United States. Once in the U.S. they parted ways and Oskar settled in the Newark, New Jersey area where he eventually met Hedy in a German social club.

Oskar self-titled the story "The Man in the Black Fur Coat". I thought it was an odd title when I started this project but I kept it until I could think of a better one. After reading about references to the black fur coat throughout the story I understood why he did that. In the end I came to regard it as an excellent title. It became an ambiguous label or name that he adopted. It was his avatar. The coat kept him hidden. He was very proud of the nickname that people gave him because it meant for him that he was winning this game. He often referred to it as a game, a game to stay hidden, unknown and alive.

As I read the story, I kept thinking about my connection with this man. I learned that all the while he was alive, I never knew who he really was either. I could have easily called him "the man in the red house-coat". I did not spend much time with him one-on-one but now wish that I did. I can only now offer my gratitude posthumously for leaving behind this journal for me to discover more than two decades after his death.

ABOUT THE AUTHORS

Oskar Scheja was born in 1908 in Lower Silesia. He was married and had one son. Oskar joined the German army in World War II and led a platoon through several battles until his capture near Dnipropetrovs'k in what is now Ukraine. After the war, Oskar left his family and travelled to the United States in the mid 1950's. There he met another German immigrant, Hedwig Rittinghaus. The unmarried couple lived together in Newark, New Jersey, and later in Bridgeport, Connecticut. Oskar worked for many years in a machine shop in Bridgeport before returning to Germany with Hedwig in the early 1970's. He died in Vechta, Germany in 1980. He left behind a journal of his experiences during and after the war that would become this story.

Dan Chiariello was born in 1964 in Hopatcong, New Jersey. He has lived nearly all his life in Northwestern New Jersey and resides today in Sparta with his wife and two sons. The exception to this was a two-year period from 1977 to 1979 when his family moved to Vechta, Germany, next door to Oskar and great aunt Hedwig. Dan is a graduate of Drew University and works today as an independent technology consultant.

ABOUT THE COVER ART

The front cover art is an original illustration created by David Chiariello. David is the great, great nephew of Oskar Scheja, and Dan's son.

The pictures on the back cover are heirloom photographs belonging to the family of the author, Dan Chiariello. For both pictures, the photographer is not known.

CPSIA information can be obtained at www.ICGtesting.com
Printed in the USA
LVOW01s1930250515

439755LV00045B/2334/P